VANESSA HALL

Copyright © 2012 by Vanessa Hall

EMOTIONS
by Vanessa Hall

Printed in the United States of America

ISBN 9781622309245

All rights reserved solely by the author. The author guarantees all contents are original and do not infringe upon the legal rights of any other person or work. No part of this book may be reproduced in any form without the permission of the author. The views expressed in this book are not necessarily those of the publisher.

Unless otherwise indicated, Scripture quotations are taken from the New American Standard Bible (NASB). Copyright © 1960, 1962, 1963, 1968, 1971, 1972, 1973, 1975, 1977, 1995 by The Lockman Foundation. Used by permission.

Also used: The Holy Bible, New International Version (NIV). Copyright © 1973, 1978, 1984, 2011 by Biblica, Inc.™ Used by permission. All rights reserved worldwide.

Also used: The New Living Translation (NLT). Copyright ©1996, 2004, 2007 by Tyndale House Foundation. Used by permission of Tyndale House Publishers, Inc., Carol Stream, Illinois 60188. All rights reserved.

Also used: The Holy Bible, Today's New International Version (TNIV). Copyright © 2001, 2005 by Biblica®. Used by permission of Biblica®. All rights reserved worldwide.

Also used: The New King James Version (NKJV). Copyright © 1982 by Thomas Nelson, Inc. Used by permission. All rights reserved.

Book Cover designed by Susan Stanley, suz180@yahoo.com

www.xulonpress.com

Dedication

To my dad, Jewel Lockett,
whose death catapulted my faith
in the God of heaven and earth

Acknowledgements

So often in life we take the ones closest to us for granted because they consistently stand by our side, supporting and loving us. Sometimes we gloss over those special but insignificant moments to cherish their love.

I would not have been able to complete this book with any level of mental focus if it wasn't for the enormous pushes from you, Kenneth. You are a wonderful man and husband who is respected and cherished by me and our family. Thank you for giving me the environment to plug away at this wonderful feat and to see it through to completion. You are my number one man and champion. I'm so blessed to have you in my life. Now get going on your own book because I know it will be a great read.

To my wonderful son Andrew, you are the treasure I hold close to my heart. You make me a proud mom because I know you love God, your family, and you respect yourself. What more can a mom ask for in her son? Thank you for being my support in so many ways and for keeping me laughing when I try to be too serious. You told me to keep moving and I am listening to you; I'm moving – onward and upward. Thanks!

God bless you, mom. I hope you are proud of my accomplishment in completing this book. You are such a loving, giving, and supportive mom and I am proud to be your daughter. You are not only my mom but one of my dearest friends, and I thank God for your wisdom and prayers. And yes, you should be relieved to know that all those days I spent at home working have proven to be a blessing.

I love all three of you dearly!

Foreword

Drawing from a wealth of biblical insight, a depth of wisdom, and personal experience, Vanessa Hall helps us to understand our emotions, how they work, and how to manage them.

She reminds us that while we cannot be free from our emotions, we can reach the place where we can be free from their control. Enlightening and eye-opening, *Emotions* reveals twelve universal emotional factors we all experience.

Our emotions are a gift from God to us; a gift to help us experience the height, depth, length, and breadth of this colorful life on this earth.

Vanessa reveals that it is universal for everyone to experience emotional ups and downs, but that ultimately how we handle the scope of these emotions makes the difference between those who unsuccessfully engage in life and those who maximize life to the fullest.

She has seen her own share of highs and lows, so she writes rather empathetically on a level where we all can identify and understand. She has the ability to express her heart, both practically and spiritually.

Regardless of where we are on life's emotional roller coaster, I believe that the real-life examples and biblical principles found throughout this book will nudge us on to emotional health and ultimately victorious living.

Babbie Mason – Recording Artist, Songwriter, Author
Babbie Mason Ministries, Inc.
www.babbie.com

Contents

Foreword: Babbie Mason ix
Introduction xiii
Chapter 1: Loneliness 1
Chapter 2: Boredom 13
Chapter 3: Patience 21
Chapter 4: Happiness 29
Chapter 5: Rejection 40
Chapter 6: Peace 47
Chapter 7: Depression 55
Chapter 8: Guilt 61
Chapter 9: Courage 67
Chapter 10: Regret 73
Chapter 11: Fear 80
Chapter 12: Love 88
Notes 101
About The Author 103

Introduction

How do we manage the myriad of emotions we experience in life or on a daily basis? On any given day, we can be significantly impacted by emotional disturbances or elation. I would prefer to contemplate those favorable times in my life when I felt I gained ground due to an emotional experience. You know, like the experience of almost giving birth to my son on the toilet when I panicked and miscalculated labor pains for a severe case of gas. (My son, Andrew, still loves that story.) Or, remembering that Saturday evening in Dallas when my husband, Kenneth, and I took a long walk in our neighborhood. After seeing a large, unfriendly dog, I was overcome with fear. I immediately yelled at the owner inquiring if the dog understood English (or did I say, "Does the dog speak English?"). My intention in asking whether the dog understood English was to ensure that it would it stop charging toward us upon my command.

Since I am sharing, it makes sense for me to tell you about an operational procedure I had in 2011. Unfortunate medical circumstances prompt most people to experience some level of fear and anxiety, and I was one of those individuals when preparing for this surgery. While the nurse prepped me for the operation, she asked me the oddest question, "Have you removed all your clothes including your panties?" Why did she have to verify my panties so specifically? "Yes, they are off," I replied. Then she told me she wanted to make sure they were off because certain material can set afire (or become combustible) during surgery, especially nylon. When she said that, I couldn't resist saying, "Well, hot panties!" while I laughed out loud in an effort to divert my fear.

Take a moment and remember your own experiences that were filled with heightened emotions, whether they were positive or negative. We are inundated by emotions, aren't we? Life wouldn't be life if we removed any one of these pesky, fun-loving, jaw-dropping, heart-wrenching, time-consuming feelings from our life's equation. Someone said, "Life is like a roller-coaster. One day you're up and another day you're down." This classic cliché evokes clarity and truth about how we manage our emotions, and how our emotions so often manage us.

In April 2011, I was diagnosed with breast cancer and according to the medical oncologist the cancer was an aggressive type. The doctor couldn't provide specific demographics that increased or decreased the odds of a person contracting this type of breast cancer. The only exceptional data she shared with me that made my eyes perk up was the fact that the type of cancer I had was prevalent among African-American women. Not long after receiving this insidious diagnosis, fear gripped my heart so stringently that I had difficulty finding my way out of the doctor's office.

The doctor had dropped a bombshell in my lap and insisted I make some decisions about my future rather quickly. To say I was stunned would be a great understatement. I couldn't believe what I'd just heard, let alone process the reality that my health was in danger and I had to make some quick decisions. At the advice of my husband and son, I agreed to have surgery to remove the cancer. Five days later after the operation, I was in the doctor's office for a post-surgical meeting. He gave me "two thumbs up" for having a favorable future free and clear of cancer. With confidence in his voice, he told me, "Now, go live your life." But before I was ready to "live my life," I wanted him to address the new lump I discovered in the same breast after surgery. He assured me it was nothing, but given my history, he arranged

Introduction

for me to have an ultrasound as extra insurance to confirm his hypothesis. I had the ultrasound and soon learned during the visit that the radiologist didn't concur with the doctor's casual suspicion that the lump was immaterial. The radiologist requested I have a biopsy to give further explanation on the lump. A few days later, I received a call from the doctor who requested the biopsy. His message stunned me again! Because in a mild but firm voice, the doctor stated, "The report shows you have breast cancer, but it is more invasive this time." In the midst of fear gripping my heart again, I managed to recall the doctor's previous advice for me to "go live my life." Now two weeks after my first surgery, I am confronted not only with another operation, but chemotherapy and a long recovery from this difficult adjuvant therapy.

I do not believe that we are by-products of our emotions, in that our lives are not summed up by our experiences and feelings, but just the same we are emotional creatures. We are not relegated by their control like a puppet is manipulated by its marionette. Not only are we emotional beings who are subject to fear, anger, anxiety, depression, and an array of other emotions, we were created with intellect and willpower. We are dynamic beings made in the express image of God and our creative, rational, emotional, and intellectual abilities are palpable. Still, we would be hard-pressed not to think that our emotional experiences don't have profound and powerful influences on us. Let's face it; our emotions are just as salient to our life experiences as our smarts, creativity, and choices.

In fact, this book is written to bring us together about one truth which is our collective reality – we are emotional creatures living in a world filled with emotional experiences that impact our lives to a greater or lesser degree each and every day. There is no way around this truth. The goal is not to be free from emotions. The goal is to be free from their control. Perhaps, we can also agree that the twelve emotional factors covered in this book are universal realities that we experience. How we manage these emotions is the difference between those of us who live successfully versus those who barely tread life's waters.

Now, let's bear down onto these twelve emotional factors.

CHAPTER 1

Loneliness

Affected with, characterized by, or causing
a depressing feeling of being alone; lonesome

*God is faithful by whom you were called
into the fellowship of His Son, Jesus Christ our Lord.*
1 Corinthians 1:9

With over 7 billion people living on earth, we could ask ourselves, "Why would anyone be lonely?" There are enough people alive for everyone to have a family and many friends. The world is barraged with entertainment, social media, and other hi-tech mechanisms for one's enjoyment. However, if we were able to zoom into people's lives, there would be scores of individuals who are battling with loneliness. What is so peculiar about living with this emotion is that the individual doesn't necessarily have to be physically alone to be lonely. Oftentimes, lonely people have family and friends who love and care for them, but because they are emotionally distant, they don't feel connected to others. When someone expresses feelings of loneliness or aloneness, essentially, he is conveying a need for meaningful contact with other people. What the person is desirous of is to connect with someone who will be more than an occasional acquaintance but who cares about him. Loneliness isn't the same as solitude such as when an individual wants "alone" time or is seeking a "staycation" to regroup from a series of stressful moments or events.

Most of us experience loneliness at some point in our lives. It can creep up gradually over time. Loneliness is serious. It can draw a person toward depression and a sense of hopelessness. It makes a person feel empty and sad. There may have been a specific incident that happened to you to make you lonely, such as a divorce. Now you are faced with the stark reality of living at home alone – where there were two plates on the table you eat in the bed in front of the television. Where there were two cars in the garage, you have piles of garage sale items parked in the empty space.

We were not created to be alone. In Genesis 2:18, God states that "It is not good for man [or woman] to be alone." God knew Adam needed companionship on a human level even though he had permanent access to His presence in the Garden of Eden. He needed to touch someone, smile at someone and eventually share difficulties with someone who was similar to him. God knew spiritual contact alone wasn't adequate to fulfill His creation. We need interaction with one another, don't we? We are a community of people who need each other. Life is too difficult to be lived alone. We need family and friends as much as we need our careers, our wealth, and our fulfilled, personal dreams. What is having a stellar career without people who appreciate your success? How is wealth enjoyable if you don't have a family or friends with whom to share it? Who is there to care for and respect your dreams if you go at it alone? This is called isolation, which is deadening and quiet. I don't mean the kind of quiet that we rush to after a long week's work or caring for your high-energy kids. Those are responsibilities that keep food on your table and ensure your future generation is nurtured. My focus is on the sort of quiet that renders you emotionally isolated. That's the place where loneliness resides. A person living in loneliness, particularly chronic loneliness, has a choice to make as to how to address this emotional drain.

The *first option* is the person could do nothing about the problem and continue living in loneliness and isolation. Many people do just that. They have learned to cope with feelings of aloneness and oftentimes will find another person who is living in this same pain and who will enable them to be lonely. It is troubling when lonely people complain about their emotional distress but passively resign themselves to simply nursing the problem. Consequently, they do nothing meaningful to change their lonely lives and to stop being aloof from healthy social connections and relationships. If our God, who has complete knowledge, awareness, and understanding because He is Creator over all things, made provisions for Adam to have companionship, can't we learn from this and agree that loneliness is not part of God's plan for humans or nature or animals? On the contrary, all of God's creatures are part of a circle of kindred spirits – humans need humans, animals need animals, and even creepy crawlers need each other. If you live with loneliness, you would do yourself a world of good if you trust my recommendation in not accepting the first option for yourself. It is not in the best interest of your physical, mental, emotional, and especially spiritual self.

Chronic loneliness forces individuals into thinking that someone is against them and that they must learn to survive in this world alone. They tell themselves they have no one in their life; that the only person they have is their own self. Some lonely people torture themselves mentally by rehashing in their minds that people don't understand their feelings, and it's no use explaining their problem because people will only give trite opinions without genuinely sympathizing with them. People living with chronic loneliness have difficulty turning off their thoughts from what is ailing them. In their own desperate way, they can become addicted to being lonely. It's not that lonely people crave loneliness, albeit some very well could desire it, but they feel trapped and unable to move beyond it. Loneliness has become their culture; their way of life. What is quite odd about lonely people is their daily routine can oftentimes keep positive and caring people on the periphery. Instead of giving someone the comfort level to help you open up and share your feelings and concerns, or better yet, care for you, people living with loneliness oftentimes place a wall up to keep the person out of their life. Sad to say, lonely people can turn against themselves and become their worst enemy.

Loneliness can be misleading. When you are around someone who is dealing with loneliness, you might misconstrue their demeanor for depression or even a lack of mental clarity. I worked with a man whom, if you were around him for a good amount of time, you couldn't help to hear him complain constantly about his work – why his boss was unfair, how his peers were lazy, or why his drive into the office wasn't worth it anymore. There were times when he would accuse other employees of trying to sabotage his work. Ironically, he was usually professional, if he cut you some slack or he didn't gripe to you about things that frustrated him on the job. Eventually, the truth about his never-ending complaints and frustrations surfaced when he told us about his break-up with his girlfriend. This gentleman was lonely because she walked away from their relationship of ten years after giving him a final ultimatum to marry her (*this scenario is strange enough that it could warrant its own chapter*). All alone, the people in the office thought he was depressed or just grouchy. That is how loneliness works. It is misleading and can often confuse you to think the person is depressed.

An article in CharmingHealth.com illustrated how loneliness may be misconstrued for depression. "People are normally prone to loneliness or feeling lonely negativity because they expect too much from friends and family. Many times their unrealistic expectations are more than what they could reasonably expect from their relationships and this brings disillusionment, frustration, and disappointment. Apart they often misinterpret their loneliness for depression. This may make them behave in a 'depressed' manner at times and make the situation much more serious. Lonely people have been found to be very hasty in making major life decisions. Many lonely people suffer from an unnecessary sense of urgency and desperation about having to quickly establish a special confidant or partner."

This article from CharmingHealth.com reminds me of a quote Mother Teresa of Calcutta made on loneliness. She said, "The most terrible poverty is loneliness, and the feeling of being unloved. There are many kinds of poverty. Even in countries where the economic situation seems to be a good one, there are expressions of poverty hidden in a deep place, such as the tremendous loneliness of people who have been abandoned and who are suffering. As far as I am concerned, the greatest suffering is to feel alone, unwanted, unloved. The greatest suffering is also having no one, forgetting what an intimate, truly human relationship is, not knowing what it means to be loved, or not having a family or friends." Mother Teresa understood loneliness intimately as she spent much of her life in the mission fields in India caring for abandoned and lonely people.

I'm reminded of a story about Pam who had been recently laid off from her job of ten years. Pam was staring loneliness in the face because for many years she invested her time and energy into having a career. She barely spent any time building interpersonal relationships or having extracurricular activities or hobbies. She rarely talked on the phone because according to Pam, after spending ten to twelve hours a day working, the last thing she wanted to do was talk on the phone or hang out with people. This sort of isolation by choice continued until the day Pam was laid off from her job. As she packed her personal belongings, Pam recalled never once stopping to call a family member or a friend to say she had been laid off. As she walked down the hallway of her office toward the exit, a few employees saw her pass by and solemnly whispered good-bye to her.

She didn't realize her loneliness until she woke up in an empty apartment the morning after she was laid off with no one to call and with whom to share this devastating news. Pam grabbed her cell phone, scanned through her contact list, and tried to find someone to talk to about losing her job. As she laid down the phone, she began to sob at the realization of how scared she was at being unemployed and not having anyone to call on for support.

Several months after the layoff, Pam received a call to interview for a new job. And like pouring Cheerios into a bowl followed by milk to see them rise to the top, Pam was up and energetic, ready to "get her life back." The interview was going quite well until the interviewer asked, "How do you have fun? We like people who enjoy life because we believe if they enjoy themselves outside of the job, they will bring that enthusiasm and energy into the workplace. And that is very important to this company as we like to have fun!"

HAVE FUN! Pam's mind made a 180-degree switch from feeling good about her chances to sinking into a dead pond of lifelessness. "Fun," she thought. "I haven't had fun since I left my last job." She slumped in the chair. She shuffled the paper in her lap. She gasped for air, "Well, I haven't had time to have other interests outside of work because my previous job was so demanding. It would be nothing for me to work 50 to 55 hours a week, and sometimes on the weekend. However, I am a fun-loving person on the job. All of my friends still work at my old company and they'll confirm how much fun I am." As she left the interview, Pam began to rehearse in her mind how unfair it was for the interviewer to ask a question about her personal interests. "It's none of their business," she thought.

A few weeks later while Pam was in her small apartment nursing her loneliness – life as usual – she received a letter from the company with which she had interviewed. The only portion of the letter she locked eyes on were the final two sentences, "Thank you for your time. We regret to inform you that we have chosen someone else who is better suited for this position." "I bet you do regret it. I do too," she thought.

Pam's story paints a general picture of lonely people who are trapped by this emotion without knowing how to get off that deafening roller coaster. And what is uncanny about a person like Pam is she thinks someone else is at fault for her misery or that people (such as the interviewer) are insensitive for intruding into her broken life.

Do nothing about your loneliness and the lonely roller coaster keeps moving. Say nothing and no one will know that the ride is killing you. If you keep thinking "when will this ride end?" but you stay on it, then you'll have to deal with the volatility of the ride. Do yourself a life-changing favor. If you are lonely, relegate it to only a part of your life, not your entire life. I know it is wiser to tell a lonely person to get some help, reach out to someone who cares, or get involved so things can get better. But the reality is if you're chronically lonely most likely you don't have the energy or interest in speaking up, let alone becoming active. That is why you should not allow this negative emotion to lord over your entire life because it has no way of helping you:

feel better

look better

think better.

Otherwise, loneliness will cripple you. And, at some

point, you'll be at your wit's end trying to find a reason to smile or get out of bed. If you isolate yourself from others socially, emotionally, spiritually, physically, or intellectually, you hurt yourself. If you ride the lonely roller coaster and do nothing about it, you hurt yourself. And both of these approaches just flat-out stink!

You can do nothing about the problem and continue living in loneliness and isolation. Well, that just doesn't work for me. I hope it doesn't work for you either. You can accept this option if you want to, but I'd strongly suggest that you don't do it. The consequences could cause you continued sadness or even depression. You could end up having suspicious thoughts about other people, believing no one cares and that life is unfair.

Make a move; tell the roller coaster engineer of your mind that this ride is over! No one can stop the ride for you unless you let them or unless you help them. The *first option* is to do nothing about your loneliness.

The *second option* is pretty straightforward. Try Jesus! That's the second option. Two words: T-r-y J-e-s-u-s!

It's my suspicion that you'll agree with me, depending on how long it takes you to see progress in this area. You will progress! This step is tried, tested, and proven. That's because I have applied it in my life. I have learned firsthand that it works. That's all it takes to get the lonely roller coaster to stop. Jesus stopped my topsy-turvy ride, and He can stop yours too. Jesus promises us in Matthew 11:28 that He would give us rest from our burdens if we come to him weary or loaded down with trouble. And let me tell you, loneliness is a burden. Trying to grapple with the harsh isolation and cruel emptiness it brings is no way for any person to live. I feel somewhat discouraged thinking about the millions of people in this world, let alone those in my sphere of influence, who are lonely. If Jesus is willing to give you rest from loneliness, why not accept it? Let Him have it so you can rest from your loneliness. Every time you embrace your loneliness, you're working in the wrong direction. When you embrace God's rest, you're ceasing from the work. Rest and don't work! Since, you are unable to remove the loneliness that is ruling your world, unload it into God's mighty hands. I'm quite sure that if you could get rid of it, you would have taken care of the problem already. Try Jesus! That's the *second* but best *option*.

Someone will critique this section and wonder why I didn't suggest Jesus first and do nothing second. There's only one reason I can provide. Lonely people have a tendency to make excuses for themselves, and if not excuses, they like to play the blame game for their misery. But once they come to the realization that they own their loneliness then Jesus can deliver them. He softens the heart so that it is receptive to His divine touch and makes the mind open to His Spirit.

Here is a simple remedy for you to consider if you are dealing with bouts of loneliness or live in chronic loneliness.

1. **Begin and End Your Day with Prayer and Pray Throughout The Day.** Don't think too much about why this will or will not work for you. This remedy will cost you nothing and save you a lot of time and effort. You may not want to invest your time and effort talking to God for long periods of time during the day. So whisper a prayer any time you need to tell God how you feel. What is important for you to feel better is to devote quality time in God's presence often and daily while you work through it.

If your loneliness is chronic and has begun to spill over to depression, prayer is essential to your mental stability. However, you should also take this emotion seriously and seek professional support to ensure you can recover some semblance of a healthy and "normal" lifestyle. Some people are reticent about visiting with a professional for emotional concerns, but I would highly recommend it particularly if Christ-centered and Bible-based advice and support are offered.

2. **Read Psalm 139 Often.** May I give you a word of caution? If you read this passage once a day or every other day, this pace isn't as effective for stopping the roller coaster as reading it several times a day while the jolting is occurring in your life.

I recommend this chapter because it is equipped with messages from God that can give you food for thought about your situation. This psalm can bring you face-to-face with the God who knows how to speak your language in helping you overcome this debilitating emotion. If you wonder whether your life matters, let this chapter sink into your heart and you'll be pleased to know how very much it matters. If you feel a distance between you and God, meditate on it and your heart will be drawn toward His love. Start today and read this chapter often and consistently.

—PSALM 139

O Lord, you have searched me and you know me. *You know when I sit and when I rise; you perceive my thoughts from afar. You discern my going out and my lying down; you are familiar with all my ways. Before a word is on my tongue you know it completely, O Lord. You hem me in—behind and before;*

you have laid your hand upon me. Such knowledge is too wonderful for me, too lofty for me to attain. Where can I go from your Spirit? Where can I flee from your presence? If I go up to the heavens, you are there; if I make my bed in the depths, you are there. If I rise on the wings of the dawn, if I settle on the far side of the sea, even there your hand will guide me; your right hand will hold me fast. If I say, "Surely the darkness will hide me and the light become night around me," even the darkness will not be dark to you; the night will shine like the day, for darkness is as light to you. For you created my inmost being; you knit me together in my mother's womb.

I praise you because I am fearfully and wonderfully made; *your works are wonderful, I know that full well. My frame was not hidden from you when I was made in the secret place. When I was woven together in the depths of the earth, your eyes saw my unformed body. All the days ordained for me were written in your book before one of them came to be. How precious to me are your thoughts, O God! How vast is the sum of them! Were I to count them, they would outnumber the grains of sand. When I awake, I am still with you. If only you would slay the wicked, O God! Away from me, you bloodthirsty men! They speak of you with evil intent; your adversaries misuse your name. Do I not hate those who hate you, O Lord, and abhor those who rise up against you?*

I have nothing but hatred for them; I count them my enemies. Search me, O God, and know my heart; test me and know my anxious thoughts. See if there is any offensive way in me, and lead me in the way everlasting.

You are NEVER alone!

CHAPTER 2

Boredom

Is a state of malaise, close to anxiety,
characterized by a feeling of emptiness

Whatever your hand finds to do, do it with your might, for there is no work or thought or knowledge or wisdom in Sheol [pit or grave], to which you are going.
Ecclesiastes 9:10

Do everything without complaining or arguing.
Philippians 2:14

Boredom is that annoying and self-centered emotion that can't mind its business and keep to itself. It has to announce how the day is a boring drag; that there's nothing on the boring TV. At work, it complains to co-workers about the tediousness of the job. And oftentimes, it results in wasting time at work on water-cooler talk, texting, or daydreaming just in an effort to not be bored. This emotion has its favorite seats in schools, usually at the back of the room, near the door. It hangs out frequently with students who aren't motivated by their academic performance. Boredom is the reason that some teachers' daily lesson plan lacks creativity to challenge students' intellect. Where there are too many external stimuli or not enough internal stimuli, there is boredom. I think that is why stay-at-home-moms take time out with organizations like MOPS (mothers of preschoolers) and MOMs Club to keep boredom away. This pesky emotion nags at people who have too much downtime on their hands or desire a shift from the routine. With the advent of technical gadgets like smart phones, cable TV, Pandora radio, Skype, and a plethora of other hi-tech devices to keep us from being bored, how is it that we are still bored?

Let me admit it my fellow Facebookers. One of my pet peeves is when someone (let's call her Girlfriend) posts a message on her page giving everyone the right to see it, stating how bored she is but she wants you to send her a private note through her Inbox with a reply. This cracks me up. Seriously! "I'm so bored, hit me up in my Inbox" or "BORED" or "This day is long and boring, Inbox me." You mean to tell me you want your friend to send you a private note via your Inbox acknowledging your boredom instead of replying to the public post you made? What's the point? The secret is out now, everyone knows you're bored. Although I'm poking a bit of fun at people on Facebook who post about their boredom publicly, but want private attention, it really is a reflective microcosm of how unrealistic and shallow we can be.

There was a recent article called *The New Resilience* in Psychology Today that broached how work-related boredom can be stressful and is a growing epidemic in our society. The article states that "Workplace boredom can be as stressful and damaging as overwork—perhaps more so. Sometimes it creates embarrassing situations, as it did for Joel, a mid-level executive. He felt so bored that he snuck out of his office one afternoon to see a movie. When it was over, guess whom he ran into coming out of the same theater? His boss!" If you've been feeling bored with your work or career, you're not alone.

Curt W. Coffman, global practice leader at the Gallup Organization confirmed, "We know that 55 percent of all

U.S. employees are not engaged at work. They are basically in a holding pattern. They feel like their capabilities aren't being tapped into and utilized and therefore, they really don't have a psychological connection to the organizations." The article includes a similar report made by the renowned Human Resources research organization, Corporate Leadership Council. They "surveyed 50,000 workers around the world" about their level of satisfaction on the job and found that "thirteen percent or 6,500 people were dissatisfied and bored." In another similar survey conducted by Sirota Consulting LLC, they report that "of the more than 800,000 employees at 61 organizations world-wide, they found those employees job satisfaction a low 49 out of 100 and those with too much work at 57." Sirota's chief executive, Jeffrey M. Saltzman, states the statistics reveal that when a person is bored on the job or in his career, this is "one of the biggest contributors to work-related stress even in today's environment of economic downturn and career uncertainties."

Boredom doesn't only cause a person to be unproductive at work. It can also be the culprit for illness due to work-related stress produced by boredom. The article noted that up to "70% of all illnesses are rooted in stress, and much of that is workplace-related. It results in $300 billion in lost revenue and $200 million in lost workdays. Whether you are an employee or employer, boredom hurts. It casts a pall on the whole organization and creates a demoralized, de-energized atmosphere," says Saltzman.

I came across another report in USAToday.com about the top reasons why teenagers engage in drug and alcohol use. The report revealed that "If parents want to reduce the chances that their teens will use drugs, alcohol or tobacco, they should keep three rules in mind: Don't let a teen get too stressed, make sure he stays busy, and don't play Santa with spending money. More than half (52%) of teens are at risk for substance abuse if they have any one of three risk factors:

stress, frequent boredom or too much spending money," according to a study from the National Center on Addiction and Substance Abuse at Columbia University.

If there is one place where boredom should be ousted it is in the lives of Christians. At best, theirs are lives of spiritual promises and fulfillment, of alms and volunteerism, of spiritual growth and knowledge, of praise and worship, and – last but not least – of fellowship and spiritual retreats. Christians believe they should be upbeat and fully engaged in life because this is what makes the world go 'round (and I've seen many Christians who are pleasant enough that the world is rotating nicely on its axis). There is an unspoken understanding among Christians that the best way to share one's faith and one's Jesus with someone who doesn't espouse Christianity is with passion and positivity. "No one wants to serve a boring God and socialize with His boring believers," is the position of many Christians. This prevailing message swirls about in many venues within the Christian community. I think this self-same message about being upbeat, fully engaged, passionate, and positive ought to undergird every social and political organization as well as all of academia. Why? This message works!

About six years ago, I received a phone call from one of my sisters who wanted to brainstorm the different possibilities for her to "have something to do," according to her words, "with her life." The kids were all grown up and had their own lives and she had recently gone through a break-up with her long-time boyfriend. While my sister was relating all the reasons why she felt she needed a change in her life, I sensed she wanted to simply say, "Vanessa, my life is boring and blasé." I felt her frustration. We tossed around several ideas for helping her find a reason to get out of bed in the morning. None of the ideas we established to counter boredom were time-consuming and difficult, but interestingly, all of them would require my sister to invest time in someone else. These suggestions wouldn't necessarily change her life immediately; however, with different engagement and a new "lease" on life, she would start feeling more energetic and positive.

Toward the end of our conversation, I asked if she'd prayed about the changes she needed to make in her life. This question didn't catch my sister off guard. She is a born-again Christian who has been in a love relationship with God for decades. She has prayed for me and with me many times. She didn't forget who she was in God. She was struggling to adjust to the myriad of negative changes in her life. I gave her kudos for recognizing the signs of boredom and taking the initiative to do something about it.

People who live in glass houses should not throw stones. That is why I am being cautious when I say "Christians who live a hum-drum with no-icing-on-the-cake life" are denying themselves the true joy of Christ expanding their horizon and getting them out of the rut or the hole they have dug for themselves. We all recognize that there are times when we need encouragement in the midst of a challenge, particularly when we need a lift to combat boredom. However, during our challenges, boredom should be the exception not the rule for living a Christ-focused life.

The Apostle Paul recognized that a Christian's life does not revolve around satisfying one's self. The Christian walk is not self-centered. It is Christ-centered. If boredom is the biggest problem in a person's life, then he is outrageously blessed beyond comprehension. There are millions of people who would love to trade places. That is why the Apostle underscores this reality in Galatians 5:17. He notes, "For the flesh sets its desire against the Spirit, and the Spirit against the flesh; for these are in opposition to one another, so that you may not do the things that you please."

This passage makes a presupposition that those who are inclined to accept this wisdom are people who have a relationship with Jesus Christ and who are filled with God's Spirit. Another observation about this passage is in order to understand the opposition between the Spirit versus the flesh, a person must be under the Spirit's control and familiar with differentiating spiritual versus non-spiritual desires. And just in case there is confusion about these two natures, Paul spells out many desires that fall in the Flesh Nature category in (verses 19 to 21) versus those in the Spirit Nature in (verses 22 and 23). Let me give you an illustration of how boredom and living in the flesh is a negative recipe.

Summer had arrived and school was out. The teenagers in AJ's neighborhood were hanging out around their homes during the day, having fun riding their skateboards and playing basketball at the nearby park. Their summer routine had kicked into high gear. For the ones who were familiar with the neighborhood and residents, AJ noticed they were leaders to the rest of the teenagers. Bryan was the oldest teenager, the one who was most familiar with everyone in the neighborhood and the most likely candidate to be the top leader of the group. Bryan would influence the younger boys to ride their skateboards in the middle of the street against oncoming cars. AJ asked Bryan why he would encourage such dangerous behavior with the kids. He shrugged his shoulders with nothing more than, "We're just bored. We want to have fun." Nearing the end of the summer school break, AJ was walking in the neighborhood and he noticed Bryan coaxing a young boy to grab his skateboard, jump on it as a car was passing by, and grab on to the car door. Instantly, AJ ran to the scene to stop the boy from going through with the plan. No sooner than AJ grabbed him from jumping onto the skateboard, the car changed lanes and almost hit the boy. Bryan stood nearby speechless. To justify what had just happened, he explained to AJ that he was just having fun, that he and the other guys were bored but he didn't mean for anyone to get hurt. Sometimes we might think that our flesh is not all that bad. In the words of Bryan, we find ourselves thinking, "We're just bored and want to have fun." Incidentally, this is the type of thinking that can create a bigger problem and lead us into paths of unrighteousness.

When dealing with boredom (or any other emotion), if a person lives by the Spirit, he will experience victory from its control. Samantha's bout with boredom led her to binge eating until she went to the doctor for a physical and learned she had high blood pressure. The doctor told Samantha to lose 25 pounds through exercise and diet, and to stay away from certain foods. The medical diagnosis was a wake-up call because Samantha had lost her mom a few years earlier due to heart-related problems. And she believed God had given her advance notice that He would bless her efforts to improve her health if she changed her eating habits. She had to address her boredom in order to make better food and lifestyle choices. Samantha's story and decision to follow wise counsel resembles a person who was led by the Spirit and not the flesh.

The Spirit desires for us and produces in us spiritual fruit, "love, joy, peace, patience, kindness, goodness, faithfulness, gentleness, self-control; against such things there is no law" Galatians 5:22-23. These nine fruit are given to us as *qualities* of God's character and are not *works* we achieve through our own efforts. No good quality comes from our flesh nature; rather, the Spirit imparts these nine qualities to yield in us a godly lifestyle, godly behavior, and godly thinking. This idea correlates with the following mathematical expression:

Holy Spirit + Spiritual Fruit + a Yielded Life − Human Effort = a Godly Lifestyle

It doesn't matter the emotional concern. It could be as simple as boredom or as complicated as living with hostility. The course of action for receiving help from God is identical. There must be a sincere interest in living by the Spirit, and desiring the qualities (*fruit*) of the Spirit. Then God will begin to produce His fruit in your life. You must continue to live according to Galatians 5:25 that encourages, "If we live by the Spirit, let us also walk by the Spirit." Then you will witness a switch from walking in your own ways (*the flesh*) to walking in God's ways (*the Spirit*).

Boredom is a growing epidemic in our society that is forfeiting people from living productive and happy lives. While boredom might not be as critical as anger or depression, it has the capability of being just as detrimental. It shouldn't be underestimated or overlooked. Although its negative effects are often time-consuming, we have a surefire way of addressing it if we live by the qualities of God's Spirit.

Boredom isn't the end of life; get engaged!

CHAPTER 3

Patience

The quality of being patient, as the bearing of provocation, annoyance, misfortune, or pain, without complaint, loss of temper, irritation, or the like

> *Better a patient person than a warrior, one with self-control than one who takes a city.*
> Proverbs 16:32

When I was a young mother my lifelong love for sleep intensified. Sleeping twelve to fifteen hours was just what the doctor ordered. My body craved it. And it was what I took great pleasure in doing. Like most young mothers, I dreaded to hear my baby cry right at the time when I was about to doze off to the tune of my own lullaby. "Oh no! Okay, I'll be extra still and quiet and maybe he will go back to sleep," were my wishful thoughts. But most of those times, that's not the way it would turn out. His cry for attention often got louder and more stubborn. There were many nights I would find myself peeking over at the clock only to realize it was just eleven o'clock. Yet the lure of sleep would send me right back to my treasured place until my persistent baby started crying again for attention. Invariably, I would tell myself, "It's too early for him to wake up. That last bottle of milk must not have been enough to keep his little tummy full." I would eventually peel myself from my well-nestled pillow and comfortable position to drag myself over to his crib. But it rarely failed. As I approached him, the crying would stop.

I will never forget those dreary nights when I looked into the crib at my baby boy lying on his back, legs up in the air, t-shirt disheveled, pamper half-way off his bottom, and looking at me with a great big smile on his stinking cute face. Within weeks, I began to reason with that boy. "Is mommy's little boy playing jokes? You were crying like your pamper was double-loaded and your tummy was on empty. And now you're smiling like a Cheshire cat. Come on little one! I'm so tired. Just close your eyes and go back to sleep." This sort of cat-and-mouse play carried on for months when Andrew was a baby. And I never got used to it. In fact, I would impatiently take care of his needs then rush him off to sleep. That was my modus operandi for many months. When the crying and play didn't stop, I began putting baby cereal into his milk so we could sleep longer.

In retrospect, while taking you down my memory lane, it occurs to me that at times, I was a selfish and impatient mom who didn't enjoy the innocent and frolicking nature of my little baby. Those eleven o'clock late night cries and sudden outbursts of giggles and smiles didn't register to me as a young mother as opportune times to love on my baby and play along with him. Those precious moments passed by quickly.

Many people carry on in life similarly to my impatient way of being a young mom. When challenges arise, the impatient person tries to hurry things along. This type of person isn't interested in learning the meaning of the challenge nor is he particularly fond of the annoyance it brings to his life. You will notice an impatient person will become irritable, frustrated, angry, or even hostile when he has to deal with challenges. My little baby, as much as I loved him, was causing me to lose sleep. And what did I do? I was irritated and annoyed, and I tried to fix the problem fast by adding cereal to his milk so he [we] could sleep longer. Well, that's the way impatient people behave. They

Patience

try to fix the challenge quickly by glossing over the details in hopes that it will go away. They get frustrated and try to instruct someone else's behavior in order to change the situation instead of changing their own actions so that they can better handle the problem. Frequently, you will hear impatient people saying, "Why did they do it that way" or "That wasn't a smart decision" or "Come on already, I don't have time for this."

Life has an uncanny way of assisting us in becoming patient. Oftentimes, the work is done without our direct knowledge. Every time there is a problem in our life, patience will automatically try to be present and support us through the ordeal. It wants to partner with us. However, we won't become patient by spending time mulling about trying to figure out why we're having the problem or how we can fix the circumstance quickly. We can't:

outthink

outsmart

outwit

our way to being a patient person. On the contrary, in order to become patient, a person must learn how to handle the challenges he faces with wisdom, calmness, and backbone. It's that straightforward with regard to becoming a patient person. If you shift your focus from trying to hurry the matter along to how you are handling the problem, you are pacing yourself to becoming a patient person. Are you being wise in how you address your problems? Are you acting calmly in the situation? Do you have the backbone to preserve in the matter? Answering "yes" to these questions poises you for patience.

Some people say the more problems or challenges you face the greater the patience. What if we change that statement from "the more" to "the greater variety"? Patience isn't developed because of the number of problems we face. That could simply mean we are hard-headed or slow to learn or just stubborn. We simply haven't learned life's lessons. And we end up repeating the same ol' problem.

A case for patience could be made for the person who keeps facing the same challenges. If the person allows himself to learn from the ordeal, he could become very patient in that particular area of his life. He may have learned to be patient in that one area only. But doesn't he want to be patient in other areas and have this same success throughout his life?

A person who was once impatient should understand how stressful it is to handle a problem without the discipline and wisdom that patience brings. He appreciates taking a step or two back to reflect on the situation, or to refrain from launching into action or speaking quickly before it's time. The former impatient person relishes learning from his past mistakes instead of walking in them in his present life experiences. The quantity of problems does not make you a patient person any more than jumping off a high building gives you Superman-like powers. It just doesn't work that way. Becoming patient is found in "the greater variety" of challenges we come up against in life. We benefit in how we effectively handle those challenges. This is what makes us successfully patient.

Here are practical examples of the "greater variety" we experience in our daily lives:

- To be tolerant with the kids, but irritable with your co-workers yields a score of 1 for patience and 1 for impatience.

- Having road rage when you're driving but tolerating

your wife's constant warning about how fast you drive yields a score of 1 for patience and 1 for impatience.

- How about waiting an hour to see the doctor who forgets to say "thanks for waiting" and you moved right past it. This yields 1 for patience (congratulations, you're a very patient person), but scolding the waiter for taking too long to serve your food yields 1 for impatience.

That's how some people work – patient in one area but impatient in another. We all need "the greater variety." When you are challenged across the breadth of your life experiences and you learn the lessons, you become a patient person through and through.

Where there is a patient person, I believe there is the Holy Spirit. It is not in our nature (*the sinful human nature*) to automatically be tolerant, patient, and enduring. Romans 8:6-8 illuminates how the sinful nature operates. "For the mind set on the flesh is death, but the mind set on the Spirit is life and peace, because the mind set on the flesh is hostile toward God; for it does not subject itself to the law of God, for it is not even able to do so, and those who are in the flesh cannot please God." Our human nature doesn't walk parallel with our spirit nature; they walk perpendicular to one another. When there is an opportunity to show patience and you don't, but instead you react in a negative fashion, your human nature is controlling you. During the times when you are patient because you have asked the Spirit to help you, your spirit nature is in control. To paraphrase God's infallible word, letting your nature control you yields death. Letting the Spirit control you leads to life and peace.

The book of Romans is unrelenting about our nature,

painting a perpetual state of hostility between it and the Spirit. There is never kinship between the two natures because our sinful nature has never obeyed God's law and it never will. But you might say this is an example of our nature and not patience. I want to know how to become patient. Yes, this passage peels back the layers of why a person is impatient. Being patient isn't just about enduring a long ordeal or tolerating offenses. Those examples represent how you handle the situation, but the heart of a patient person is about what is controlling you. Is the Spirit controlling you? Is your sinful nature in control? Patience comes from the Spirit. And to be patient, the Spirit must have control. That is why those who are still under the control of their sinful nature can never please God.

Galatians 5:22 supplants any idea that patience is not a Spirit-thing. It is integrally part of God's Spirit, making it a quality (also known as "fruit") inherent to God alone. God will gladly produce this quality in a person's life. And the good news is there is no need to beg or plead with Him for it. The Spirit delights in producing it in us so that we patiently behave, think, and speak like Him.

John 15:8 declares that "My Father is glorified by this, that you bear much fruit, and so prove to be my disciples." If you want to be patient, you can be patient. Jesus confirms this by telling us that it brings God glory when we bear not just fruit but much fruit. In other words, we are overflowing with good qualities. This is a sign that we are His disciples. I love this passage! It gives me confidence in my prayers when I ask God to produce His patience in my life. Since I know it gives Him glory, I know He will do it. And it gives me great expectations of inheriting more of Him in me.

The power of John 15:8 is real in my life. During the time I was writing this book, Kenneth and I had to visit the radio station to complete some production work for *Grace Matters*, our weekly radio program. We walked to the conference

Patience

room with our account manager. We were introduced to the producer who was assigned to work with us. After we made our introductions, the producer asked our account manager what we planned on producing that day. "Nice," I thought. The account manager clarified the objectives and we went to the production room with the producer. While preparing to record the program, the producer received several spur-of-the-moment, work-related messages, which forced him to multi-task between completing those requirements and working with us. Other radio employees interrupted our recordings that caused him to leave the production room to assist them while we waited or recorded solo without him. After an hour of interruptions and not much progress, the producer said he had to leave and pick up his child from school. The time came for us to talk with the producer about the additional work needed to be done during the production session. Upon learning the extent of our production needs, he announced that he wasn't aware of the scope of services we required. However, he let us know that we should focus on the most important areas and arrange for another visit to complete the balance.

While the producer was out the room handling some other business, Kenneth and I warily locked eyes. We were clearly thinking identical thoughts except Kenneth blurted out our sentiments, "This visit isn't as smooth as I would imagine. They don't seem to be on the same page." And just like any other aha moment, we took a deep breath while Kenneth reminded us that "we are teaching others about God's grace. So, this is a prime opportunity for us to be graceful to the radio people while we iron out the wrinkles." I sighed with comparable conclusion as I sensed the Spirit echoing this same sentiment in my heart. "I agree," I told Kenneth. But what was uncanny about all of the interruptions and miscommunications was that I was right in the middle of writing this book and working on the chapter of patience. God never misses an opportunity to give us great teaching moments. It's us who often miss them. He has a way of producing patience in us without always using critical measures. Our scenario wasn't critical in the grand scheme of things, but we had to quickly corral our thoughts and emotions because as things were progressing, it could have been a perfect situation for conflict to arise.

If you are an impatient person, if you desire to be more patient, or if you are already patient, believe God to empower you with John 15:8 and you will abound in patience.

> Go ahead, trust God to give you patience;
> it brings Him glory!

CHAPTER 4

Happiness

The quality or state of being happy

When times are good, be happy; but when times are bad, consider: God has made the one as well as the other
Ecclesiastes 7:14

If God asked you to sell all you own and give it to the poor, do you think you could be happy with losing your creature comforts? This question should remind you of the story in Mark 10 when the Rich Young Ruler approached Jesus to ask him how to inherit eternal life. Jesus of course pointed him to God and told him to keep the Commandments. The Young Ruler fared well in these areas. He told Jesus he was on par with keeping the law. Then Jesus told him to "sell all his possessions and give his money to the poor, and he would have treasures in heaven." After the accomplishment of this selfless act, the Young Ruler was directed to follow Jesus.

This is where we run into the problem with the Young Ruler. He was willing to follow Jesus up until the point where Jesus wanted him to sell his creature comforts and turn his wealth over to the poor people. Apparently at that moment of challenge, his wealth meant too much to him to forfeit, even for the sake of eternal life. Did he really want to be saved? Or was he cautiously ignorant to what it would cost him?

Now notice what happens to the Young Ruler after Jesus

gives him more directives about inheriting eternal life. First of all, what I can tell you is he was not a happy man. He didn't find a state of happiness nor any quality of it after Jesus told him to give his earthly wealth to the poor. Consequently, that young fellow made a choice against inheriting eternal life because he was not willing to give up his wealth, and it made him sad. That is what (verse 22) says about his frame of mind, "When the young man hear this, he went away sad because he had great wealth." How is it that the Young Ruler initiated the conversation as he appeared to be moving strategically toward another successful story? He wanted eternal life and he knew Jesus was the way in which to obtain it. My mom used to tell me, "If you don't want to know the answer, don't ask the question." Mom is right. The Young Ruler asked a loaded question for which he was not prepared to hear the answer. Ultimately, he kept his possessions but it cost him.

I can't think of any solutions, remedies, panaceas, etc., for making a person happy outside of having a relationship with Jesus Christ. I simply can't find another viable way! If you were offered wealth would it make you happy? Would fame, power, influence, or beauty make you happy? Oh, I know. What if you didn't have to work any more and had enough money to live a fun and full life? Then, would you be happy? What could someone offer you that would give you happiness? Some wise guy is reading this section and thinking he could find much happiness in many of the situations I posed. He is saying, "I would take any one of these offerings in a heartbeat. It's more than what I have now and I could do a whole lot of good with these blessings." On some level, I believe I could be happy too if I had wealth or influence. Most women might certainly attain a level of happiness if they had beauty. What woman among us doesn't want to be beautiful?

If you weed through the details of this story, you should

find yourself staring in the face of someone who couldn't resist coveting wealth. He loved his wealth more than he loved poor people and God. He was quite successful in keeping the letter of the law. It wasn't the letter that severed his happiness. It was the Young Ruler's unwillingness to love the spirit of the law. Jesus wasn't broke. He wasn't after the Young Ruler's money nor was he trying to hit him where it hurts. Jesus was offering him eternal life and being the all-knowing God (Jesus), He knew the Young Ruler needed to sever himself from his wealth. It wasn't the amount of money with which Jesus had problems. In fact, the verse doesn't focus on how much the Young Ruler was worth. Jesus wisely honed in on a critical truth that this man didn't see. What are you holding on to for yourself that you are not willing to give to Jesus? This question was the crux of the matter because it pointed the Young Ruler to the spirit of the law which is to "love the Lord your God with all your heart, soul, strength, and mind," Luke 10:27.

A person might enjoy levels of happiness throughout different times of his life. However, if Luke 10:27 isn't dancing in your spirit, chances are you will not be able to sustain this happiness. As a matter of fact, a person who is moral but not necessarily committed to God is not excluded from enjoying the happiness that God brings. Happiness is a universal emotion and whoever wants it goes after it. Vocalist and conductor Bobby McFerrin wrote the 1988 hit song, "Don't Worry, Be Happy." It was the song that brought him worldwide recognition. Most people don't remember much about the song except for the part when he whistles to the backdrop of that bouncy reggae tune. Or when he sings the phrase that everyone loves and remembers, "Don't Worry Be Happy." Bobby McFerrin's song tapped into the heartbeat of people around the world. And the truth is it is inherently in our souls to be happy.

The righteous can't complain when the wicked are happy,

and the wicked can't protest that the righteous are happy. In Matthew 5, Jesus silences this sort of sparring with the righteous against the wicked. Jesus reminded the people that they were taught to love their neighbor and hate their enemy, then He offered them a new principle whereby to live. He admonished them to love their enemies and pray for those who persecuted them. The reason for this new principle is found in verse 45: "so that you may be sons of your Father who is in heaven; for He causes His sun to rise on the evil and the good, and sends rain on the righteous and the unrighteous." In other words, Jesus was saying evil and unrighteous people are recipients of God's universal blessings that His children also enjoy. What do you mean evil people are blessed? Yes, God allows His blessings in the lives of evil people. God has a way of giving us shock treatment, doesn't He?

This Matthew 5 principle wouldn't have sat too well with Jeremiah, the fiery Old Testament prophet. He had witnessed enough prosperity among non-God fearing people and a whole lot of suffering and fear from God's children – so much so that it drove him to complain. In Jeremiah 12:1, he spoke his complaint to God like this, "Righteous are You, O LORD, that I would plead my case with You; Indeed I would discuss matters of justice with You: Why has the way of the wicked prospered? Why are all those who deal in treachery at ease?" This prophet had seen one too many evil persons. He was fed up with their so-called happiness. "God, but what about your children," Jeremiah probably lamented. Oh, you better believe God hasn't forsaken his children's happiness. Non-righteous people enjoy happiness in the here and now ONLY, but God's righteous people not only enjoy it now but for all eternity. I am not smart enough to understand why someone wouldn't want Jesus. He controls our current existence and He is awaiting us beyond this life. The fullness of happiness is intrinsically available for God's children.

Bobby McFerrin should have titled his song: *Know*

Jesus, Be Happy. And that upbeat, whimsical whistle would have inspired more people to not only tap their feet and bob their heads but would have also imparted a spiritual truth in their hearts and minds.

So, did you answer the question that kicked off this chapter, "If God asked you to sell all you own and give it to the poor do you think you could be happy with losing your creature comforts? If I had to answer this question three years ago, my immediate thought would have been a resounding "no." I wouldn't be happy. But God hadn't molded my life back then the way He has so lovingly done over the last three years. He has proven to me, even though He doesn't owe me anything, that He is a faithful God. He's credible in my individual life experiences. Today, I would say "yes." I believe I could be happy without my creature comforts. What about you? Has God made Himself known to you in ways that your faith in Him supersedes your comfort in what He's blessed you to have? I hope so!

While there is no formula for happiness, and you cannot buy happiness, and given happiness is a state of mind, I would like to entice you into wrapping your minds around nine spiritual principles for being happy. Now remember, happiness is more than acquiring "things" and "stuff." Untold numbers of people have tried that and are still not happy. It is time to try a new approach that is tried, tested, and approved by Jesus. He introduced the nine beatitudes in Matthew 5 and they revolutionized the disciples' thinking way back then. And they are still revolutionary in this modern age.

Happiness 1 | *Happy are those who are poor in spirit (humble) for theirs is the kingdom of heaven.* The happy person is one who realizes that he cannot save himself and recognizes his inability to elevate himself with God. He understands his own sinfulness and his need for God's grace. Unlike the spirit of the proud, a humble person doesn't regard his status. Instead he seeks, like the beggar he is, help from God. I believe this spirit of poverty is a prerequisite for acquiring the other eight beatitudes.

Happiness 2 | *Happy are those who mourn for they shall be comforted.* How is it possible for mourners to be happy? That is a promise that only Jesus can deliver. Bible scholar Matthew Henry provides commentary on this type of happiness. He states, "It is a result of godly sorrow which works true repentance, watchfulness, a humble mind, and continual dependence for acceptance on the mercy of God in Christ Jesus. This is accomplished through constantly seeking the Holy Spirit, to cleanse away the remaining evil. Heaven is the joy of our Lord; a mountain of joy, to which our way is through a vale of tears. Such mourners shall be comforted by their God."

Happiness 3 | *Happy are the meek for they shall inherit the earth.* I think the third beatitude is the most offensive when stacked up against the world's system. Our society pushes for self-confidence and self-assertion, not modesty, gentility, or compliance. All of these words are negative and can lead to low self-worth, according to today's conventional wisdom. Television media and school systems in particular are inculcating the message that self-expression and self-adulation are valuable qualities in our world. These public influencers don't necessarily juxtapose these attributes against qualities such as meekness or humility. However, the pervasive message is communicated loudly that a person won't succeed, won't be accepted, or will be deemed weak or inferior if they portray themselves in any way other than self-confident. The siblings to self-expression and other popular self-centered perspectives are entitlement and obtaining "my rights." Our society is saturated like a soggy dishcloth with people who feel they can have whatever they want, when they want it, and how they want it. Their basic premise that cradles this "me-centric" mindset is "if not me, then who?"

Now contemplate what Jesus is telling us about the kind of people who will inherit the earth. And you should see the difference between those who are meek versus those who are "self-centered," as well as those who will inherit the earth from those who will not reap such a blessing.

John Gill's *Exposition of the Entire Bible Commentary* gives us a great explanation of the quality of meekness. It states, "Here meekness is to be considered, not as a moral virtue, but as a Christian grace, a fruit of the Spirit of God; which was eminently in Christ, and is very ornamental to believers; and of great advantage and use to them..." Meekness isn't just being humble or gentle as in a moral virtue, but it is a fruit of the Spirit of God. You can't be meek unless God produces this quality in you. It is God-centered not self-centered.

Gill explains that the meek shall inherit the earth is "not the land of Canaan, though that may be alluded to; nor this world, at least in its present situation for this is not the saints' rest and inheritance, but rather, the 'new earth', which will be after this earth is burnt up...only such persons as here described shall dwell. And who shall inherit it, by virtue of their being heirs of God, and joint heirs with Christ, and the fullness thereof." I believe Gill hit the nail on the head in stating the reward for the meek. They will be rewarded a place in the new earth.

Happiness 4 | *Happy are those who hunger and thirst for righteousness for they shall be completely satisfied.* Food is one of my all-time favorite subjects. It is quite common for me to plan my meals in my mind and salivate on the visuals as though I was chewing the real thing. This happens particularly often when I'm dieting. I can get lost eating my mental meals; food stays on my brain when I diet. This beatitude conjures thoughts of an exquisite meal and beverages for people who are looking to be satisfied for pursuing righteousness. I'm curious about what's on the menu and what beverage is served. Certainly, it has to be yummy! Let's go and dine on this promise.

Jesus strategically located his teaching spot for the Sermon on the Mount (in which the beatitudes were delivered) in Galilee on an elevated, mountainous area where He could sit in reasonable proximity above the crowd yet close enough for them to hear. What a smart move on Jesus' part. For rest, fresh air, and open space, Jesus found his spot. For nourishment, strength, and pleasure, He chose food and drink as his attention-getter.

The explicit visual for understanding this beatitude's meaning is your body needs food and water for nourishment and survival. If you don't supply its needs, you will eventually die. And eating one time isn't enough to live, nor is it possible to remain healthy and productive if you eat a few times a year. The body needs ample nourishment every day. What is true for the body is true for the soul, and Jesus nailed this point so brilliantly. The message is if you want spiritual nourishment, if you are feeling lost as a sinner and strongly desire to be righteous, if you know your soul is suffering from malnutrition, and your heart is brittle and parched from thirst, seek God. Go after the things that are important to Him. Make it your business to be astute in His Word. Go for broke in petitioning Him to feed your hungry soul. Then your soul, your life, will be satisfied. He will serve you the finest, most exquisite meal your soul has ever eaten.

Happiness 5 | *Happy are the merciful for they shall obtain mercy.* In many inner cities across America there are communities of homeless, poor, and needy people living out in open spaces. Some are there by choice and others are not; life just happened to many of them. These indigent people are probably in the same boat as many who are living in the suburbs in their nice homes, driving their fine cars, and having a plethora of resources, but whose life is burdened by addictions or abuse. I can't imagine what would make a person who is living in an abusive home or strung out on drugs better than the person's situation who has nothing and is living on the streets. Frankly speaking, both are in need of mercy.

For better or for worse, this beatitude partners with the adage *actions speak louder than words* when showing mercy for a person's physical and spiritual needs. Everyone has his own burdens to bear. Yet, the standard for obtaining mercy is to show it. We are called, even created, to bear one another's burden and pain. And we must do all we can to help people who are in need. Giving alms of mercy seems far better for the giver than the receiver. That is why God blesses the giver when he shares his compassion and pity for others. People who might not deserve mercy but are in need of it might not appreciate your kindness or forgiveness, but God does. You will receive mercy. He promises it! Your acts could be the very thing that God uses to help someone get out their situation or even more, bring them into the Light of Christ. Someone said, "Sharing one another's joy is double joy but sharing one another's pain is less pain."

Happiness 6 | *Happy are the pure in heart for they shall see God*. It has been said that there is a way to determine if a person is good. You must observe their behavior or listen to what they say. The problem with this type of litmus test for good folks is you can't prove they are good just by what they do or say. They might be a phony. Conversely, there is a surefire way for you to know if your own heart is pure before God. A pure heart is the quality of life that will get you face to face with God forever. It is no wonder Jesus said, "A pure heart" because this heart represents His heart for the world. You are pure before God when your motives and actions are the same toward God and others. That is when you love God with all your heart, mind, soul, and strength, and love your neighbor as yourself. This is a pure heart!

Happiness 7 | *Happy are the makers and maintainers of peace for they shall be called the sons of God.* Do you resemble God? Do your peacemaking ways parallel His? Wait! Don't answer the next question if you are not confident that God's peace saturates your life. Are you living a quiet and peaceful life that satisfies God? You have permission to skip right over this question if there are doubts in your mind that your life is at peace with God. If you don't have peace with Him chances are your life isn't all that happy or peaceful either. He is the God of peace and every believer of Jesus Christ can and should live peacefully. John 14:27 reminds us of this fact when Jesus said, "Peace I leave with you; my peace I give to you. Not as the world gives do I give to you. Let not your hearts be troubled, neither let them be afraid."

The whole premise behind this beatitude reveals a chain reaction between God giving us His peace and us successfully living at peace with one another. I Corinthians 14:33 declares that "God is not a God of disorder but of peace." And those who promote peace like Him are called His children.

Happiness 8 | *Happy are those who are persecuted for righteousness' sake for theirs is the kingdom of heaven.* In our so-called postmodern society, it is becoming rapidly unacceptable to say "God" at public events yet it's even more contentious to say "Jesus." There is growing hostility against individuals who profess faith in God through Jesus Christ. The world hates Jesus and this isn't a surprise to Him or His believers who know what the Bible says about Jesus' reputation in the Last Days. "If they hate me," Jesus said, "they will hate you."

We are not asked to voluntarily seek persecution. That is not smart. On the other hand, if a believer suffers for lifting up the name of Jesus, standing up for his Christian faith, refusing to participate in non-Christ-like activities with un-Christ-like people, to name a few examples, he should be happy. This is the Christ-like persecution about which Jesus says, "Do not fear those who kill the body but are unable to kill the soul; but rather fear Him who is able to destroy both soul and body in hell," Matthew 10:28. God's Kingdom belongs to the believer who doesn't run toward persecution but allows his light to shine in this dark world even if that means being persecuted.

Happiness 9 | *Happy are you when people revile you and persecute you and say all kinds of evil things against you falsely on my account.* Can Jesus' warning of reviling (condemning or censuring), persecuting (discrimination, bullying, or killing) and speaking evil of righteous living be more relevant than living in this 21st-century, global community? We are there folks! Christian values and lifestyle choices are taboo nowadays. Evil has taken center stage in the hearts of people who reject Jesus and his followers. The Bible is replete with warnings and admonitions about these last days (which is known as the timeframe from Jesus' ascension until he returns to earth a second time), so that Jesus' followers can act wise as serpents but harmless as doves. We are not called to go after the persecution. We are called to stand firm and fully committed in the face of persecution on account of Jesus.

> Since we are forgiven and saved,
> we can be happy!

CHAPTER 5

Rejection

To refuse to accept, acknowledge, use, believe;
to throw out as useless or worthless; discard

*However, those the Father has given me will come
to me, and I will never reject them.*
John 6:37

A soldier was serving overseas and far from home. He became upset when his fiancée wrote breaking off their engagement and asking for her photograph back. He went out and collected from his friends all the unwanted photographs of women that he could find, bundled them together and sent them to the ex with a note that read: "I regret that I cannot remember which one is you. Please keep your photo and return the others." Although I am not certain this story is true, it does hit at the heart of what happens to us when we face rejection.

This soldier's rejection caused him to retaliate against his fiancée. Most likely he trashed her out with all those friends who loaned him pictures. She didn't know it, but because of the rejection, her would-be husband revealed that he would have been the kind of spouse who would seek revenge or retaliation if things didn't go his way. Although the soldier deserves sympathy for the heartbreaking disengagement note, the fiancée did herself a favor when she stumbled upon a weakness that could have been a culprit for future marital problems. He gets an "A" for being a soldier and serving his country. But he'll not escape with a grade above an "F" for dealing with rejection negatively.

The soldier is not alone in how he handled the rejection, is he? Nope! Most people would like to think they can handle rejection in a sophisticated or level-headed way. Before the rejection occurs, we might think if a certain scenario happened in our lives, we would do this or do that. We rely on our reasoning to persuade us in taking the high road without getting sucked into an emotional abyss. But, unfortunately, the 'this' or 'that' usually translates into retaliation, revenge, depression, or some other negative emotion that hurts our cause. And when it's all said and done, sophistication and level-headedness were merely concepts that eluded us.

Rejection is a heart-wrenching, off-putting emotion that is not easy to deal with or from which to recover. Did you notice the definition of rejection at the beginning of the chapter? It means to *refuse to accept, acknowledge, use, or believe; to throw out as useless or worthless; discard.* Now keep this definition in the forefront of your minds as I share what happened to the brain in a study called "**painful-rejection**" conducted by Edward Smith, psychologist, and other colleagues from Columbia University in New York City, according to the National Geographic Daily News, March 28, 2011.

The report revealed that past studies on rejection "have shown that simulated social rejection may be connected to a network of brain regions that process the meaning of pain but not the sensory experience itself. However, in this newest study, MRI brain scans of people jilted in real life show activation in brain areas that are actually tied to the feeling of pain," according to Edward Smith. Participants reported, "going through an unwanted romantic relationship breakup within the past six months." The participants "were asked to look at photographs of their ex-partners and think about being rejected. When they did so, the parts of their brains that manage physical pain—the secondary somatosensory cortex and the dorsal posterior insula, to be exact—lit up," according to the study.

"The study isn't a true perfect experiment because Smith couldn't control who had the rejection experience and who didn't. Yet, the results are striking," Smith said, "especially because the team analyzed 150 other brain-scan experiments on negative emotions—fear, anxiety, anger, sadness—and found that none of these emotionally painful experiences activate the brain's physical sensory areas in the same way as an undesired breakup. There may be something special about rejection."

According to the study, the brain is challenged to recognize the line of demarcation between rejection and pain. It would have been informative and possibly beneficial for Smith and his colleagues to study how long it took these participants to recover from the rejection as a result of their romantic breakup.

Research shows that people who handle rejection quickly can recover from it more effectively than those who allow it to eat away at their life. Because festering can lead to blaming yourself for the other person's decision to hurt you, causing you to feel shame and guilt, or, even worse, making you depressed or neurotic. Before you get a grip on the rejection, your problem morphs into something bigger because you are still holding on to it. Wasn't it bad enough for the person to reject you, let alone for you to hold on to that pain?

If you are struggling with rejection as a result of a family crisis, job loss, divorce, discrimination, numerous failures, or any other negative actions or actions you perceived to be negative, how long will you allow it to cast a stronghold on you? I realize letting go of the pain carries a myriad of considerations. You might have to speak with someone who can coach you away from the pain; rally around close friends

Rejection

who will give you positive reinforcement and prayer; remove yourself from the painful environment; get the courage to face your fears and the person who rejected you; ask God for wisdom to forgive the offender, or learn to respond appropriately to the rejection. To remain silent and passive is a recipe for internalizing your rejection and compounding your problem. Then, the domino effect kicks in to your life because your rejection becomes condemnation, insecurity, suspicion, or other self-conflicting behaviors.

Is rejection ever justified? Perhaps I can interject my opinion based on my past work-life experiences. I have been laid off from three of the five professional jobs that I've held. The timeframe for these five jobs spanned across six years. And I am certain the other two jobs would have phased out if I hadn't voluntarily left before I received the ax. From my five job experiences, it seemed as though right at the time I became acclimated to the job, built relationships, and things were going well, my name would surface on the layoff list or the company was buzzing about impending layoffs in my department. There wasn't a problem with my performance or relationships, but because of the nature of my former profession – Human Resources/Organizational Development – my job was highly expendable. Without fail, the reasons my employers stated for laying me off was budgetary constraints or a change in corporate vision. You would think those business reasons would assuage my hurt of the rejection, but they never did. From one layoff to the next, I began to believe that there was something wrong with me; that I was marked like a bull's eye. For three years, I feared going on job interviews and it hurt to talk about my past work experiences. I felt like a failure. I'd see former colleagues who were working hard, being rewarded, and ascending in their careers, and then I'd compare myself to them and wonder what my career would be like if only I could have kept a job.

At some point in those three years of living with rejection and submerging my feelings, I began to think God had rejected me too. Prior to those thoughts, I had felt that since He had the power to change my situation, He would do it. He knew how hard and dedicated I was to my work. After praying for years and eliciting other Christian family and friends to join me in prayer about landing a job, I reconciled in my heart that God was working against me too. And as God's child, when you ascribe blame to God about your difficulties it is nearly impossible to walk by faith. This is how rejection manifests itself. If you don't deal with it quickly and honestly, you will bow underneath its control. You begin to blame others, blame yourself, and live in self-pity. Instead of God opening the door for me to return to a traditional job in Corporate America, He chipped away at the feelings of rejection in my life through giving me opportunities to hash out my feelings and hurt in a safe and private way, speaking to me in my quiet prayer and study times, placing people in my life who cared about my situation, and showing me His will and desire for my work life. He proved to me that He loved me; that He wasn't against me but He was for me. As such, God showed me that I was against myself. He convinced me and I began my road to healing.

My encouragement to you is that if you are dealing with rejection you will benefit greatly if you saturate your mind with the Word of God. Among many great passages, I believe Hebrews 4:15 can support you through the pain. It teaches us that "For we do not have a high priest who cannot sympathize with our weaknesses, but One who has been tempted in all things as we are, yet without sin." Jesus understands us. He sympathizes intimately with our rejection. What's more, we can be assured that if we imitate His actions and reactions we will handle rejection successfully. Left unchecked, rejection will conquer our minds, emotions, and spirit. Jesus' life was marked by rejection – Isaiah 53:3 says that He was

Rejection

both despised and rejected of men. He, our great High Priest, relates the matter of rejection personally and convincingly to the Father.

Another passage that I would recommend you saturate your minds with if you're dealing with rejection is 2 Chronicles 16:9. It says, "For the eyes of the LORD move to and fro throughout the earth that He may strongly support those whose heart is completely His..." Imagine what this passage is asking you to focus on. There is not a day that the sun rises where God is not actively involved, intervening, or initiating on behalf of His children. Why is He so involved in His children's lives? The verse states He is actively involved to strengthen those dear children whose hearts are bent toward God. Despite the rejection, stay bent toward God. No matter the pain, seek God. No matter how low you feel, continue to be a God-lover. And He will strengthen you!

Well, three verses are a charm and I want to share a third passage that can ease your troubled mind when rejection has you down. Jesus says in Matthew 11:28, "Come to Me all who are weary and heavy-laden, and I will give you rest." This verse complements 2 Chronicles 16:9 because essentially both verses are teaching us to keep seeking an intimate and personal relationship with the Lord. If you are stressed from rejection, go to Jesus and get some rest. When your mind is in a negative place and you can't shake it off, run to Jesus and He will give you rest. If you want peace of mind, restful nights, or sunny days, go, I tell you! Go! He will give you what you need.

I asked earlier if rejection is ever justified. There's no doubt in my mind that God, Jesus, and the Holy Spirit don't operate through rejection. This would be counterproductive to their loving plan for us. My experiences have taught me while God doesn't reject us, rejection might be justifiable through the eyes of the person doing the rejecting. Nonetheless, it is rarely acceptable to the person who has to endure it. Oddly enough, those job layoffs have taught me how to be sensitive whenever I have to turn down someone's ideas or reject their behavior. My sensitivities have helped me to become more compassionate with people who are hurting because of being rejected. And I'm not so sure I could be more helpful to others if I hadn't had first-hand experiences in this area.

It has taken an enormous amount of courage for me to deal with rejection on my jobs, but it has taken a whole lot more courage to write about it and make a public confession. God has given me rest and lifted the burdens I carried and my life is much lighter.

Thank you, God – You will never reject us!

CHAPTER 6

Peace

A state of mutual harmony between people or groups, especially in personal relations; cessation of or freedom from any strife or dissension

> *Peace I leave with you; my peace I give you.*
> *I do not give to you as the world gives.*
> *Do not let your hearts be troubled and do not be afraid.*
> John 14:27

A few years ago, Kenneth and I packed the car and headed for East Texas to enjoy a weekend getaway at one of Jefferson's finest bed-and-breakfasts. While driving and enjoying the scenery, I noticed a billboard that happened to be the best visual of peace I've ever seen. It was that popular solid black, plain background billboard that you might have seen on the side of a major U.S. highway. This billboard read – No God, No Peace! Know God, Know Peace! Now, considering I'm a word nerd whose learning preference is highly visual, and given that I'm detail-oriented, this sign grabbed my attention. Someone had cleverly written an attention grabber that

The billboard I saw was similar to this visual.

accurately states the truth about peace. And I took a mental snapshot of this statement and filed it away in my memory. Without fail, every time I take a road trip, I look for those black billboards to grab my attention and give me more spiritual fodder to contemplate as I travel.

No God, No Peace! Know God, Know Peace! This is a statement that must be seen in order to fully grasp its truth. But once you see it, you get it immediately. And if you're seeing clearly and understanding well, you will buy into this statement at first glance. What the billboard's message is saying is if you don't want God in your life then you don't want peace either. However, if you want peace in your life, you also want God. But the trouble we have with this truth is many people want peace outside of God and want God without living in His peace. Either way, both of these factors are sad commentary. Think of it this way, if you are not a born-again believer, a follower of Jesus Christ, and you want a peaceful life, how will you acquire it without the Peace-Giver imparting it to you and sharing it with you?

There is a simple solution to this question, a direct way to having your cake and eating it too. Romans 5:1 teaches, "Therefore, having been justified by faith, we have peace with God through our Lord Jesus Christ." Where do you suppose the origin of peace resides? Is it a quality inherent within every person's existence? God is Peace. He is the Initiator and Giver of peace. God extends His peace to us through our relationship with Jesus. This simple but profound truth might be difficult for many people to accept, both Christians and non-Christians. Some people ask, "Do you mean to tell me that I can only have peace if I have a relationship with Jesus Christ?" Refer back to Romans 5:1 because it gives the guidelines on having peace. The passage reveals the object of our peace is in our relationship with Jesus; that is how the verse ends. We have peace with

God because of what Jesus Christ our Lord has done for us.

To this, some people might reply, "Are you saying only Christians enjoy peace? I know many people who are not Christians and they live peaceful lives without having a relationship with Jesus." We never fully understand true peace unless we know the One who gives it. Therefore, not all peace is created equal. Those people who enjoy life peacefully without God are experiencing what I consider temporal peace. Temporal peace is established on a person's standard of beliefs and how they choose to live them out.

Take the man who decides he loves his girlfriend and asks her to move in with him. After a few years of living together, they decide to have a baby together. They enjoy this type of living arrangement and feel it suits them well. In fact, the couple decided against marriage because they have low regard for God's absolute morality and for legal commitments. This couple professes to be living a peaceful and enjoyable life together without any confession of Jesus Christ as Lord over their lives. Interestingly, they don't fully grasp peace in the first place because in order to know peace, you must know God. They have determined how they want to live and have managed to keep a healthy semblance of functional peace present in their lives. At the end of the day, theirs is a temporal peace. This couple can only enjoy a degree of harmony with each other. But in terms of experiencing a greater, sustained peace with God, one that carries a spiritual harvest, one that is both for the here and now and in eternity, this type of peace eludes them.

The passage in Romans 5:1 cautions us from believing we are the originators of peace. The passage corrects this faulty way of thinking because it teaches peace comes as a result of our relationship with Jesus. It is a very difficult prospect to try and convince someone how to live a peaceful life when that person doesn't feel his life misrepresents this virtue. When the person doesn't believe having a relationship with Jesus is a requisite connection for true, life-sustaining peace, it is his choice to live without this belief. Remember, the Holy Spirit is the only one who can give true peace, and many people will decide against His idea of it. Respectfully speaking, if a person doesn't want God's peace he's not obligated to it. God won't subjugate our will or choices. He loves us too much to do so.

Now, if a non-Christian can't derive true peace from their own strength, what makes born-again, followers of Christ believe they can have God's peace without fellowship with Him just because they are His children? They can't! The criterion for having the peace of God in one's life applies both to His children and those who are not His. That same passage in Romans 5:1 finds its place in the conversation again because it reminds us that to know peace is to know God. "Knowing" God runs deeper than having an awareness of Him, being knowledgeable about Him, or even attending a Bible-based, Spirit-filled church. These are not sufficient factors for experiencing the personal, intimate, and nurturing relationship with God. He wants YOU, not what you know or what you do. His peace is attached to His relationship with you. You can't just say, "I'm at peace in my life. I'm good! I'm okay!" Your life can't be run by your strategy, desires, or control. You will never find God or His peace that way; that is, if you want this virtuous gift or if you realize you are beyond its reach, get to know Him intimately.

Is your life chaotic? Are you riding under the pressures of being a mom, husband, family member, friend, or employee? Are your frustrations and stress levels heightened? Are your life challenges bogging you down? Well, you should be assured that you can make a choice for the One who can give you true peace. He can tidy up your chaotic life. He's willing to ease the pressures of your relationships. He wants to diffuse your frustration and stress by bringing them down low. And He aims to make your steps firm and your path clear.

Tressa was a college student who would spend late nights watching TV while studying. Through her multi-sensory work-style over the course of several semesters, she found herself in a lot of trouble academically. After several semesters of following her favorite TV shows and trying to crunch for homework assignments, Tressa received her grades showing she was failing several of her classes, and was about to be placed on academic probation. The academic advisor told the young lady that she needed to find a tutor in hopes of improving her grades. But she knew she didn't have a learning concern or an inability to grasp the material. Her problem was she was a TV addict who loved hanging out in her girl-cave. Keeping up with her favorite shows was by far more exciting than biology or history. The choice, however, was no longer Tressa's if she was to continue to be a student at the college. She had to make a commitment that school was more important than her escapism with TV or she could pack up her belongings and return home. From an outsider's vantage point, Tressa's situation doesn't seem very severe in the broad scheme of life. Someone might say, "Just turn off the TV."

When Tressa received her new grades, her GPA was still lower than required for passing the semester. A few weeks later the school decided to place her on academic probation. And if Tressa was to recover from the school's severe warning, she had to demonstrate that she could keep a specific GPA for three consecutive semesters or be expelled from the school. She was crushed. Dropping out of school was not an option. She knew she could do the work, but how would she convince the school? How would she explain this matter to her parents?

One day while walking to class, Tressa saw her friend Sony. He asked her to attend chapel service with him later that evening. He told her that a very popular speaker was the guest and she was supposed to be "really good." Since Tressa was already in trouble with the school, she felt she wouldn't lose out on a thing if she joined him. Plus, she needed an emotional boost.

During chapel, Tressa kept whispering to Sony that the speaker must have been prepped by the academic advisors to talk to the students about being committed to their education and to God. She told him, "The one thing that strikes me about this message is there are over 300 students in this auditorium, and I could have sworn the speaker overheard my conversation with the advisor and was sent to chapel to tell me to get it right." Then she poked Sony in the side with her elbow before telling him, "You must be in on the plot because why otherwise would you invite me to chapel out of the blue. You've never invited me before." Then she whispered, "I can't tell you the last time I attended a church service."

The Spirit of God was moving in Tressa's heart. She responded to an appeal the speaker made about giving her life to God and allowing Him to meet her needs instead of utilizing things and people as the first option. The speaker said, "Go to God first." So Tressa did! She gave her heart to Him. Tressa said, "It was time for me to resume my relationship with God. I needed Him!"

Over the course of the next two semesters, she began to buckle down and focus hard on her studies. In the midst of her hectic school schedule, nostalgia for TV, and craving to be in her girl-cave resurfaced, but God was teaching Tressa how to recognize His peace and leadership in her life. The more she stressed over making the grades and keeping up with homework, the more often she prayed about her situation,

Peace

and the greater her awareness of God's peace continued to sweep over her life.

God's children don't have to face a precarious situation before He intervenes on their behalf. His peace is good enough for our small and seemingly minor challenges as well. He welcomes them! Unfortunately, we're the culprits in many instances that keep Him at bay during our challenges. When things get to an unbearable pitch, there we go running to our Father. Why do we wait? We know He is the God who specializes in hard things or when we're stuck on "stupid." He wants unbroken fellowship with His children. God knows that during the times we try to handle life on our own or we are passive, even lazy, about bringing our matters to Him, it hurts us. Those times cause us to feel neglected and unsettled. Deep in our hearts, we know we need God and His peace to protect our hearts and minds. We have to know the signs of broken fellowship with God, and the clues are most likely unique for each of us. This is very important for God's children to identify when they have move beyond the peace of God and to quickly find their way back to safety. Otherwise the enemy will be on high alert ready to stalk our hearts, our emotions, and minds, and try to convince us God isn't listening or we can handle it without Him. If non-Christians can't derive true peace in their own strength, what makes God's children believe they can have His peace without fellowship with Him just because they are His children?

There are many verses in the Bible that encourage us to know God's peace. For instance Luke 1:78-79 says, "Because of the tender mercy of our God, by which the rising sun will come to us from heaven to shine on those living in darkness and in the shadow of death, to guide our feet into the path of peace." These verses connect our hearts with the passage in Luke 2:14 where the heavens sang "Glory to God in the highest, and on earth peace among men with whom He is pleased." The angels filled the sky with praise to God when Jesus was born. Even the angels are convinced that God's peace is given to those whom He favors. And God favors His children.

According to the article, *Seeking the Peace of Christ Christianity and Peacemaking*, in the mid-19th century, Frances Havergal lived as a faithful and talented Christian. She wrote many treasured hymns, including *Take My Life and Let It Be Consecrated*. During her relatively short life, she was plagued by many difficult challenges. When she was eleven, her mother died. Within a short time her father remarried. Frances' stepmother came between her and her father, causing deep hurt to the girl. As a young adult, Frances became chronically ill. Even to get up from her bed was painful. Yet she continued to live actively, especially in her songwriting ministry. During one of her periods of illness, she composed these words:

> *Like a river glorious is God's perfect peace*
> *Over all victorious in its bright increase*
> *Perfect yet it floweth, fuller ev'ry day*
> *Perfect yet it groweth, deeper all the way.*
> *Stayed upon Jehovah hearts are fully blessed*
> *Finding as he promised, perfect peace and rest.*

God's children can have perfect peace in the midst of their life's difficulties, something that is beyond human comprehension. No striving for it, no begging to have it, and no worrying whether He wants to share it. He freely gives His peace to His children.

Yes, true peace is God's gift to His children!

CHAPTER 7

Depression

A condition of general emotional dejection and withdrawal; sadness greater and more prolonged than that warranted by any objective reason

Why are you in despair, O my soul? And why have you become disturbed within me? Hope in God, for I shall again praise Him for the help of His presence.
Psalm 42:5

You rarely see the listless days of depression coming. When they arrive, you want them to go away. But they won't. They zap your energy and steal your interest. They fight you, but it is an unfair fight because there are so many of them against you. All they can share is sadness, sadness, and sadness. There, when they meet you in bed as you wake up, it's another day for singing that same 'ol song: "I don't want to get out of bed. I don't care!" They move about the day with you as though you are their best friend. If, or when you eat, they invite you to binge on comfort food. They tell you, "You need a big square brownie and ice cream." And you go for it. You let your calls go to voice mail intentionally because you don't want to talk to people, even if the calls are from people who care about you. They believe they have your number too. They don't mind if you don't brush your teeth, wash your face, or shower every day; that's not their concern. They have convinced you to neglect your essential hygiene and after days and days of them hanging around, you're now a believer. You think it makes sense for you to pop a sleep aid so that you can escape their quicksand effect in your life. And so you go for it. One sleeping pill turns into a daily regime for medicating those dreary days, as long as they show up.

It is there that you find yourself tucked away in the dark chamber of depression. Those dark days have trumped your normal life. Have you ever been there? Are you there now? One day your world is as normal as normal can be. You are surrounded by the familiarity of family, friends, work, and "your world." It's your world, your comfort zone. Until something invades the familiarity of it in such a harsh and painful way that you no longer feel the need to act normal. That is when your world is no longer normal because depression has become the "new normal" way of living for you. You may not have seen it coming as an unwelcome guest in your life. Though you tried to avoid it, you felt powerless to tell it to "skedaddle, beat it," or flat out "get lost." So, don't go feeling your situation is all that unique. No ma'am, no sir! There are millions of people whose lives are being policed by that rancid magnet called depression.

Mental Health America is America's oldest and largest non-profit organization that addresses all aspects of mental health and mental illness. They "regularly conduct a variety of polls and surveys to gauge public perception of mental illness in America, and to examine trends in how the nation addresses mental health care." In ranking America's mental health, *An Analysis of Depression Across the States*, reveals that "depression is a chronic illness that exacts a significant toll on America's health and productivity." It also stated that depression "affects more than 21 million American children and adults annually and is the leading cause of disability in the United States for individuals ages 15 to 44. Lost productive time among U.S. workers due to depression is estimated to be in excess of $31 billion per year. Depression frequently co-occurs with a variety of medical illnesses such as heart disease, cancer, and chronic pain, is associated with poorer health status and prognosis, and is linked to sudden stressful events such as death of a family member, divorce, job loss, and severed relationships." The survey also revealed that depression "is also the principal cause of the 30,000 suicides in the U.S. each year."

It is my guess that the twenty-one million people reported by Mental Health America is much higher particularly since they are not able to report on the millions of Americans who don't have health benefits to be treated, those who refuse to be helped because of the exorbitant cost of medical care and prescriptions, people who are against medical help but would rather treat the sickness with natural remedies or spiritual intervention, and those who deny the severity of their condition. The prospects of how large this number could be of people suffering from depression is staggering. America has 311 million citizens and if we work off the twenty-one million alone that was reported by Mental Health America that equates to one in fifteen people are living with depression.

Chances are if you work, someone on your team is depressed. If you are a student, several of your peers are depressed. If you are a stay-home mom, someone in your mommy circle understands depression. If you play sports, a teammate or competitor is confronted with depression. Even if you are a child of God, someone in your circle is or has been dealing with depression. It is chronic and widespread, and if not handled, depression can lead to more deleterious and far-reaching concerns for the individual.

It's another fact that friends and family of an individual suffering with depression are exposed to what I consider derivative symptoms. You don't have to be the person who has depression to understand and relate to the effects of it.

You too experience the effects as you support your loved one. Any caretaker or close friend can attest that depression is very difficult to live with or recover from.

I have several close friends who have suffered with depression. Some have experienced a life crisis that propelled them into that dark place. Others who lived with clinical depression needed medical assistance, psychotherapy, and prescription drugs to address the matter. In my personal life, I struggled with situational depression off and on for two years when my work-life was in shambles. There were times when I refused to move from the bed and had to remind myself why getting out of it was important. Emotionally, I had lost my way. Through my own personal experiences and exposure to my friends' difficulties, there are five areas that I consider derivative symptoms of depression. These are areas I have experienced in being a support to my friends and they were areas in which I was affected.

SHOCK | When I first learned about what was predicating my friends' emotional upheaval, be it a chronic disease, divorce, parents who abandoned them, a cheating spouse, or losing a child, my mind was overcome with shock. I just couldn't believe they were dealing with so much turmoil. Frankly speaking, I didn't know how to deal with it either. There were times when the shock was so crippling that I couldn't even speak and my emotions were all pinned up inside. The involuntary disbelief and shock replayed over and over in my mind like a broken record, and I wished that what I had discovered was a mental mirage. Shock is what I term "the spontaneous reaction" to the discovery.

REMORSE | What can be worse than seeing your friend depressed is realizing that you can't fix his problem. There is nothing you can say or do to remove the loss or pain. There were times in my experiences where I wanted to help, but felt so helpless that I would get frustrated with myself. I soon learned that feeling sorry for my friend's loss was a sign of true friendship, and it was also an indication that my friend's problem would require someone in addition to me helping him get through the crisis.

FEAR | Whenever my friends' depression, or, for that fact, my depression, began to take on its own life – when the normal things in life were not getting done or enjoyed anymore – I found myself being fearful. Fear came when I thought my friends wouldn't seek help and could get worse. My mind would be taxed with wondering how long the crisis would last. Would they make it through it?

WORRY | On occasions, I felt my friends had resigned themselves to living with depression. It was easier to coddle the problem than to deal with what was causing it. They conveyed that they didn't know if their situation was resolvable; that "it is what it is." As a friend, that mentality worked up a great deal of worry about the outcome of their situation. Consequently, worry is what I had to carry to the Lord when my friends' depression was wearing on me.

FRUSTRATION | Depression is stressful in and of itself, and when you have a friend who is crushed by self-pity or has an excess of excuses about why things won't change or why they don't care anymore, that can be very frustrating. I'm sure a few of my dear, sweet friends felt frustrated with my shenanigans when they tried supporting me during those terrible job layoffs. Without fail though, I have learned that a true friend understands depression can be deceptive not just to the individual living it but to the support person as well. What I know today is a person can rise from depression if he is earnest and committed.

I heard someone say, "Sometimes people don't make the necessary changes to improve their life until the pain of remaining the same is greater than the pain of changing." So true!

The key scripture for this chapter is found in Psalm 42:5. The strength of this passage can soothe the feeble mind of individuals who are depressed because God cares about your depression. You can be assured that He isn't subjected to the five derivative symptoms we carry when supporting someone with depression. He is the panacea for all our cares and troubles no matter if they are mental, social, emotional, spiritual, or physical. Read this Psalm. It is soothing to an aching heart: "Why are you in despair, O my soul? And why have you become disturbed within me? Hope in God, for I shall again praise Him for the help of His presence."

Jesus came to this world to save us, reunite us, heal us, and sanctify (*consecrate*) us. John 10:10 says it this way: "The thief comes only to steal and kill and destroy; I came that they may have life, and have it abundantly." The life Jesus wants for you is in the making RIGHT NOW and will continue throughout eternity. He is there with you, giving you peace for times such as living with depression. "Peace I leave with you," says Jesus. "My peace I give to you; not as the world gives do I give to you. Do not let your heart be troubled, nor let it be fearful," John 14:27.

When living with depression, you're up some days and down other days. No matter what the mood, you must trust in the hand of Almighty God to see you through your crisis.

Grab the Word, a godly friend, and fight depression like there's no tomorrow!

CHAPTER 8

Guilt

The fact or state of having done wrong or committed an offense; responsibility for a criminal or moral offense, deserving punishment or a penalty; remorse or self-reproach caused by feeling that one is responsible for a wrong or offense

> *Can mankind be just before God? Can a man be pure before his Maker?*
> Job 4:17

    Have you ever had to have a heart-to-heart conversation with someone only to find out a secret that you wish they'd never shared with you? It sort of makes sense for the person to ask you to keep the private matter confidential. And it really makes sense for you, the listener, to keep their matter confidential even if the person doesn't say, "This is between you and me; got it?"

    Most of us know the unspoken rules to secrets. Rule One – you don't spill the beans even if it hurts your head and burns your lips. If you agreed to keep silent then you should keep your word. Rule Two – if someone asks you to keep their situation a secret from your spouse that's a problem especially if your spouse is trustworthy. I usually have to throw in my caveat after this request and let the person know that I will keep it a secret but the hubby and I don't keep secrets from each other. That said, there are times when the information isn't pertinent to the hubby anyway and he might not want or need to know. Rule Three – now that you are privy to the secret, you should analyze it to determine whether the person needs to be reported to the police, family, spouse, pastor, or someone else. I know! I know! You are screaming, "But it's a secret. How in the world can Rule One be upheld if Rule Three encourages you to, 'break the rule' if you feel so inclined?" I'm just saying there are secrets that can make you culpable to the offense. All rules are meant to be broken when it comes to secrets, especially those that pertain to crimes or moral offenses. Then you need to act fast and spill those beans! When it boils down to it, guilt acts similarly to the person confessing his secret in that it causes you to be weighed down by wrongdoing, offenses, or bad behavior.

Guilt is that emotional reaction to an offense that trumpets, "You know you shouldn't have done or said that. What were you thinking to do something like that? Why did you break those rules – you know better." Guilt is the inner voice that condemns your behavior or thinking. You can suppress the voice and eventually you might not feel guilty anymore. You might be resistant to handling the offense or seeking forgiveness, which will bode very low for your psyche and can snowball into depression, shame, or even anger.

Feeling guilty often amplifies personal shame. That is the purpose of guilt – to convict us of wrongdoing, to stop certain bad behavior that violates our conscience and others, and causes humiliation or embarrassment. When our behavior is in conflict with the convictions of our conscience, but we engage in it anyway, we are supposed to feel guilty. It is a normal reaction to wrongdoing. If a person continues to engage in wrongdoing, and his conscience continues to convict him of his bad behavior or poor choices, this will lead to shame.

Guilt

Guilt can be a corrective emotion. Think about it. If you have offended or hurt someone, you recognize it, feel sorry, and make amends; then you are able to move beyond the guilt. By the way, there are legitimate reasons for offending someone, such as reprimanding a person for wrongdoing or refusing to support a person's sinful ways without carrying the weight of guilt or shame. We are empowered by the Word to "speak the truth in love." But you must speak it.

Shame is a harmful emotion because it causes you to feel inferior, disgraced, or embarrassed. All three of these feelings are dangerous and counterproductive to anyone who wants to live a healthy and functional life. It is possible that the same behavior that caused guilt in one person can produce shame in another. Shame is the tactic abusers use on their victims to make them feel that they aren't "good enough" and not worthy to seek help.

Guilt is a good moral compass that has been used to affect social change. I believe it was guilt that was the backbone to much of the 1960s civil rights and women's rights movements. Those valiant warriors went to extreme lengths to revolutionize society's behavior and actions. Their objective was to breakthrough the establishments of America in order for them to see their wrongdoings against minorities, women, and foreigners.

From a spiritual viewpoint, we know different sins carry different consequences even though all sin separates us from God. We distinguish sin as "big" or "small", but God defines sin as "a transgression of the law." This point is taught in James 2:10-11. It states, "For whoever keeps the whole law and yet stumbles in one point, he has become guilty of all. For He who said, "Do not commit adultery," also said, "Do not commit murder." Now if you do not commit adultery, but do commit murder, you have become a transgressor of the law." James isn't promoting that a murderer is also guilty of adultery; rather, that we stand before God either forgiven or condemned. What is true for God's law is true in our American court of law. If someone is convicted of murder, he can't plead his case that he should be released because he hasn't committed theft, embezzlement, or assault. We stand before the judge either innocent or guilty. Violating even one law, though we obey the rest, makes us guilty.

Does God use guilt? I believe the answer is yes. There is biblical support for my position. God uses guilt when we have sin that has not been confessed, when there is iniquity in our lives (*or when we live in overt sinfulness*). God considers this type of lifestyle a sin problem. The Word says, "If we regard iniquity in our heart God will not hear our prayers," according to Psalm 66:18. Yet, where there is sin and guilt, forgiveness is available and ready. 1 John 1:9 provides the way for forgiveness. It teaches that, "If we confess our sins, He is faithful and righteous to forgive us our sins and to cleanse us from all unrighteousness." Jesus reinforces this teaching in John 8:36, "If the Son sets you free, you will be free indeed." Once we confess our sin, the buck stops there because that is the time you must not engage in that sin again. God uses guilt to convict us of iniquity, which is considered a lifestyle of wrongdoing. However, He doesn't use guilt or condemnation to remind us of our past sins. He doesn't need to because now we are living righteously before Him. Our lifestyles are pleasing to Him. The Word supports this when it teaches there is no condemnation to us if we are in Christ Jesus. So you ask, "Then why do I still feel guilty if God has forgiven me?" In a few words, "you haven't let it go." Knowing you're forgiven and feeling forgiven can be diametric opposites. This simple truth has become many Christians' Achilles heel in terms of trusting God to keep His promises.

I'm reminded of a story about Hardin, who rarely speaks up for himself. It was another long night on the job when Hardin started surfing for pictures of nude women. As

Guilt

was his pattern, Hardin would ensure his employees were bogged down in work before he would shut his office door and wander off into his own sexual escapade for hours. This risky activity on Hardin's part went on for more than six months. It wasn't that Hardin was "bad," but he was trapped in passivity over his addiction and felt shame to reach out for help. His wife had confronted him a few months earlier about his addiction and Hardin assured her he had stopped.

On a particularly long night at work, Hardin was tucked away in his office indulging in his recent trend of pornography. When someone knocked on his door, it was one of the Information Technology (IT) guys reporting that some of the servers had been infected by a virus and they needed to check all the computers. While the IT guy waited for Hardin to let him in the office, he glanced at the computer and noticed the images on the screen. "Uh, Hardin what are you doing, man? All I can see are naked ladies." Hardin's head dropped, his pupils dilated, and his heart started racing. After Hardin lost his job, his wife encouraged him again to get help for his problem. She told him he needed to give that sin problem over to God; otherwise, it could ruin their marriage.

It was three months later when Hardin and his family was at church that he approached the pastor, asking him for help with his addiction to pornography. Through many long and trying months of hashing out his feelings and behavior, Hardin became convicted that his problem was too big for him to solve and that God wanted to deliver him. The guilt and shame he felt lingered long after he had asked for forgiveness and stopped the illicit activity. Hardin didn't speak up about his guilt and shame. He merely coped with it. Then one day while in counseling with his pastor, Hardin confessed that he would never feel forgiven by God if the images of pornography and his desire for it didn't disappear from his mind. The pastor explained that it would take time before the images and desires were completely erased from

Hardin's memory. Then he firmly stated that they might never completely go away. "Nonetheless," said the pastor, "you must not fall back into that pattern of living." He reminded Hardin that even though he didn't feel forgiven that God had forgiven him. The pastor's instruction was to not yield to temptation, even though Satan was harassing his mind and making him feel guilt and shame. He challenged Hardin, "Remind yourself of God's promises that declare you are forgiven and not condemned."

You too may not feel forgiven, but if you have confessed your sin and turned away from it, you are forgiven by God. This reality bears more truth than your feelings that are making you feel guilty. As God's child, hold on to what the Word says about you even if you're staring at thoughts and feelings that are opposite. God's Word is our eternal truth for our present life and our future life in glory.

You are not guilty in Jesus Christ!

CHAPTER 9

Courage

The quality of mind or spirit that enables a person to face difficulty, danger, pain, etc., without fear; bravery

Be strong and of good courage, do not fear nor be afraid of them; for the LORD your God, He is the One who goes with you. He will not leave you nor forsake you.
Deuteronomy 31:6

Jesus Christ, Abraham Lincoln, Mother Theresa, Winston Churchill, Harriet Tubman, the Pilgrims on the Mayflower, Corrie ten Boom, 9/11 Rescue Workers, Martin Luther King, Jr., Anne Frank, Christopher Columbus, Susan B. Anthony, and Martin Luther the Reformer.

Thirteen Names – Thirteen Individual Causes – Thirteen Sacrifices

How is it that these people's legacies need no introduction; that their influence still reverberates in our world today, and their life contributions changed the way we live in one way or another? How can these illustrious people stand alone on their own merit with just a mention of their name, and we clearly recognize their value? What is it that these people have in common?

Emotions

They are Courageous Giants

They possessed a formidable courage. They usurped fear and defeat. They were mighty warriors for their individual causes leading the way to a better humanity. *In memoriam* to all thirteen individuals who lived courageous lives and died champions; their legacy lives on. In the case of Jesus Christ, God raised Him from the grave and He is in heaven at the right side of the Father. Hallelujah, Jesus Lives! From one life to another, across their broad spectrum of passion and mission, our world has been <u>phenomenally</u> impacted by their courageous character. And the world has never been the same.

We often decide people are courageous in hindsight. The truth is we were created with the ability to take that first courageous step and move forward to challenge our own fears and doubts. For some people, courage is as simple as saying, "I'm sorry" or difficult as being on the front lines in a battlefield. Courage comes into play when ethics, morality, or spirituality is on the line, and you must stand up for your beliefs or a cause. Courage is doing the right thing even if right is difficult without fear of public opinion or personal gain. This is the kind of courage Jesus demonstrated throughout His life and at pivotal moments such as in the Garden of Gethsemane, before Pontius Pilate, while the jeering crowd screamed, "Give Us Barabbas!" at Golgotha, and hanging on the cross.

If I could bring this chapter to life, courage would undeniably be the formidable character trait, the innate emotion that propels lives beyond the status quo. It would be the one voice that screams, "You can do it!" Courage is the chapter that is seeking readers who are willing to stand up in the face of fear, carry on bravely, and trust in God's providential plan – NO MATTER WHAT! This chapter implores you to have courage.

Courage

In one of the most intense scenes in the movie *Courageous*, the fourth film produced by the Media Ministry of Sherwood Baptist Church in Albany, Georgia, a man was at a gas station when his truck was stolen. The thief began to peel away but not before the man reacted by grabbing hold to his truck while the thief dragged him down the road. As the man held onto the door for his life, he fought the thief with all he had. Oncoming cars flew past this pursuit. At one point, the door flung open and the man dangled from the truck as a fast-moving eighteen-wheeler barreled down the one-lane road. As a viewer, your inclination is to scream, "Let the door go! Don't be a hero and end up dead!" Instead the man fought the thief until he forced him to drive the truck off the side of the road. By this time, policemen arrived at the scene and worked quickly to apprehend the thief. As the policemen secured the perpetrator, the frantic victim quickly jumped into the truck to check the condition of the true source of his emboldened response. Unknown to onlookers and those who had just arrived on the scene, the perpetrator had been traveling with precious cargo – the man's baby boy. He grabbed the baby and held him to his chest with a thankful sigh of relief.

There was no question in the man's mind why he was acting with reckless abandon. Hanging on the door of that truck for dear life meant more than just recovering a vehicle. It was the difference between knowing someone has just kidnapped his baby and taking decisive action or simply standing by and doing nothing. Even if the man hadn't been successful in rescuing his boy, his actions epitomized courage. He had heart! His heightened sense of emotions propelled him to act bravely in the face of danger.

In an April 28, 2011, Psychology Today article by Dr. Stephen Diamond, he expounds on this formidable strength. He defined courage as "standing up to evil and fighting for what we truly believe in takes moral courage, especially when it places one's own physical safety or that of one's family at risk. Spiritual or moral courage is what allows us to acknowledge our human failings, weakness and fears, and accept rather than conceal them behind a facade of macho bravado or spiritual pretension. Paradoxically, it can be a courageous and encouraging act to confess our vulnerability, sensitivity, anxiety or despair to others." It is in a person's spiritual DNA to be more than a survivor; we are born to be courageous.

The Apostle Paul is without doubt one of the greatest Christians to ever live; all Christians since him have benefited from his Spirit-filled ministry and life. When Paul was on his way to Damascus to undertake another murderous campaign against Christians, Almighty God intercepted his plans by blinding him with a bright light and instilling a type of fear in him that forced Paul to renege on his original strategy. From that experience until Paul's death, he availed himself of spiritual faith and courage to endure a life of unending suffering. Paul didn't rely on self-help courage to defeat his challenges and live circumspectly before God. Instead he said, "I can do all things through Him who gives me strength," Philippians 4:13. He rejoiced in the power of Christ in Him. By that example we know that we too have access to the same spiritual power and courage.

We live in a society where postmodern thinking and beliefs have insidiously inculcated almost every area of life around the world. Postmodernism is an ideology that is in opposition to commonly and traditionally held beliefs, practices, ideas, or knowledge. This ideology is in a perpetual state of evolving to something better, moving away from tradition, or fighting against the norm even if it means paradoxically opposing its own ideas. Satan has used postmodernism to remove prayer and the Bible from our schools. He's empowered political leaders to refute the Ten Commandments and their unerring truth upon our courthouses by getting rid of them. He has made it more difficult for Christians to share their faith in these places once considered common ground for speaking about one's belief in Jesus Christ. Now the postmodernists have dubbed our society as post-Christian. And their ideas have gained great popularity. Christianity is rigid, myopic, insincere, exclusive, and intolerant to repeat a few terms echoed by postmodernists. They insist on political correctness, moral relativism, and a no-way-is-better-than-another approach to faith. Satan has made it more difficult for Christians to stand up for their faith in many parts of our society. It is not comfortable or acceptable to share one's faith evangelistically. It is not risk-free to buck the crowd, social mores, or the current fads. One would say it is easier to go along with the crowd. However, Christians are people who are empowered by the greatest force ever known to man – the Holy Spirit. God's Spirit gives us courage to face these societal challenges and changes in our world.

As time nears an end for Jesus' second coming, we must rely on the Holy Spirit to accomplish His work in us because evil is ever present and with greater intensity. Our courage of faith is steeped in knowing "Greater is He who is in [me] than he who is in the world," 1 John 4:4. God is greater! Postmodernists' agenda is seemingly triumphant in our world with all its anti-Christian and post-Christian sentiments and beliefs. But, Christians, let us not forget they are taking on a 100% fail-proof Kingdom agenda. The Bible says to them, "No weapon that is formed against you will prosper; and every tongue that accuses you in judgment you will condemn. This is the heritage of the servants of the LORD, and their vindication is from Me," declares the LORD," Isaiah 54:17. That is why Satan is working like gangbusters to deceive as many people as he can. His goal is to try and annihilate the cause of Jesus Christ through God's children because he knows his time is nearing an end.

Be courageous in your faith by being true to your Christian principles and beliefs. You are making a difference in this world. No matter what opposition we face, Christians must continue to light up this world with the love of Jesus, brighten the corners where we live, and have positive influence for righteousness' sake.

You courageous Christian you!

CHAPTER 10

Regret

A sense of loss, disappointment, dissatisfaction;
A feeling of sorrow or remorse for a fault, act, loss, regrets;
A polite, usually formal refusal of an invitation

> *...I do not consider that I have made it my own. But one thing I do: forgetting what lies behind and straining forward to what lies ahead, I press on toward the goal for the prize of the upward call of God in Christ Jesus. Let those of us who are mature think this way, and if in anything you think otherwise, God will reveal that also to you.*
> Philippians 3:13-15

People have said to me, "If there's one thing that I regret it is 'such and such'. If I could take it back, my life would be much better than it is." People who contemplate their past and feel a sense of loss or disappointment are living with regrets. And whether or not a person is ready to move beyond his past suggests he is cognizant of the problem. Unfortunately, just because a person is aware of regret, this knowledge doesn't change the problem. There's no way around the fact that the source for regret is not a safe place at which anyone should camp. At best that place is dangerous for any healthy mind and is the culprit for needless

Emotions

time spent feeling guilty. As painful as the past might be, the past is the past, and it won't disappear from your mind if you waddle in its memory.

During those times when your mind is reminiscing on past hurt and disappointments, that is when you must remember to create a mental power surge. Turn off those negative and painful thoughts then find an outlet to plug in thoughts that will lift your spirit and give you encouragement. If you won't change your thinking who will? You might say, "God can change my bad thinking even if I can't." He most certainly can change our thinking with or without our assistance. He's Almighty God. However, God's method for changing us is very similar to a man taking a woman on a date. When he arrives at her home, he gives her a flower not because she can't buy herself a flower, but because he is a gentleman. He opens the car door for her as he takes her to a very nice restaurant and fun movie not because her hands are tied and she can't open the door for herself, but he is a gentleman. When the night is over, he walks her to the door and waits until she closes it just to be on the safe side, not because she doesn't know her way to her front door, but because he is a gentleman.

That is exactly what God wants from us. He can erase our bad memories and regrets, but He wants us to bring them to Him so He can have ownership of them. He won't usurp your free will or yank your regrets from you unless you give Him permission. He is the Gentleman God who created us with the ability to do much more than that for which we give ourselves credit. If we partner with Him by turning over the matter and leaving it under His control, He will leave a beautiful flower of peace with us. He will open the door of our hearts to surrender even more than we originally gave Him. He will carefully watch after us by shielding our minds.

It is one thing to feel regret, but it is entirely another matter to allow regret to overtake your mind. Isn't it enough that you were hurt by the past experience? Why exacerbate your pain by holding on to what has hurt you the most? Let me remind you of the overarching theme of Chapter 9, which is courage. And courage is demonstrated best when we do the right things even if right is difficult instead of doing what is easiest, despite public opinion or our own personal gain. The theme, courage, dovetails well with helping people who are strapped in past memories and need to become free.

Essentially, there are two factors that cause people to regret a past experience. These factors revolve around a bad choice the person made or a bad situation that was imposed upon the person against his will. Aren't these the same two factors (*choice* and *force*) that have paved the way for much debate over how we were created in the first place? There are many people who appreciate the fact that God created them with the ability to make their own choices. They enjoy the fact that they are not robots or puppets on a string. That God doesn't micromanage their thoughts and decisions from Heaven. "Having a choice," they would say, "is God's gift to humanity." I too stand with those people on the side of choice. Life would be unbelievably mundane if God dealt with us like programmers operate a robot. All that would be left to enjoy would be an unattractive and boring life. It's even conceivable that we would be hard-pressed to find a reason to continue loving God.

Like those people who appreciate freedom of choice, there are others in the debate who intonate that they would have preferred it if God had created them like robots or puppets on a string. They might say, "Making a decision would be much easier." If God micromanaged life, if their thoughts and decisions were cookie-cutter ready, they wouldn't have to live with regrets. Their choices would already be prepared for them. And what is more, everybody would make right decisions all the time because we wouldn't have a choice in the matter. Life would go God's way all the time. It is an amazingly powerful reality that the All-Wise God chose to create us with the ability to choose and think freely, not by forcing us into submission. He created us to make any choice whether for Him or against Him, or about anything else in life. God knew that by creating us this way we would also need the ability to utilize our minds freely whether for good or bad.

I am not the only one who appreciates how God created us because David declares his respect in Psalm 139:14, "I will give thanks to You, for I am fearfully and wonderfully made; Wonderful are Your works, And my soul knows it very well." Here David is heralding God for His brilliance with which He created us. He is making a fuss over God's wonderful ways because David states, "Your works are wonderful. I know that full well." David respected God's choice of creating us as free-thinking beings with the power of choice.

In another passage in Psalm 8:5-8, David serenades God for creating us in His image and giving us dominion over the earth. In this serenade, he states: "Yet You have made him a little lower than God, and You crown him with glory and majesty. You make him to rule over the works of Your hands; You have put all things under his feet; all sheep and oxen, and also the beasts of the field, the birds of the heavens and the fish of the sea, whatever passes through the paths of the seas." No blessing other than Jesus dying for our sins is greater than being created in God's image. Genesis 1:27 expels any notion that being created with freedom of choice was a mistake because the passage declares, "God created man in His own image, in the image of God He created him; male and female He created them." Finally, along comes verse 31 that places a heaping pile of icing on the cake as it reveals God's pleasure in how He created us. The Word declares that "God saw all that He had made, and behold, it was very good. And there was evening and there was

Regret

morning, the sixth day." How can we who are created in the image of Almighty God, who have dominion over the earth, whose excellence prompted God to say "It is very good" live with regrets?

Fortunately for Paul, he understood how living with regret got him nowhere and that it isn't God's Will. That is why he states, "I do not regard myself as having laid hold of it yet; but one thing I do: forgetting what lies behind and reaching forward to what lies ahead, I press on toward the goal for the prize of the upward call of God in Christ Jesus. Let us therefore, as many as are perfect, have this attitude; and if in anything you have a different attitude, God will reveal that also to you." Preach on Paul! This verse speaks with elevation like the band high-stepping across the football field showing off their moves at half-time. Paul is high-stepping across these passages with the kind of talk that makes the rubber meet the road; he's getting down to the bottom line of living in a forward-motion life, with no regrets. There are three principles revealed in this passage that can propel us from living with regret to being revitalized.

Principle One | It won't come as a surprise to you when I say, "You are only alive by God's grace." Good health, exercise, healthy eating, taking natural herbs, or "living green" might support a great quality of life, but all these remedies combined plus a great amount of others won't sustain your life when God says, "Your time on earth is done." Because of this point, Paul owns up to the fact that his righteous living or his devoted commitment to God was not the source for obtaining the great prize of salvation when in actuality Jesus was the reason. He was still in pursuit of a more righteous life that he knew could only be obtained through God's Spirit. Paul was a man on a mission!

Perhaps, unlike Paul, there are days when you feel the odds of progress are stacked high against you. When there is a place to coddle your regrets, you find yourself curled up there because it is that sort of "I feel sad" time. I think it is in those moments we are nearer to the heart of God than when we are content. Take the time to reflect but never let it be an occasion for falling back into a mental quicksand over what went wrong in your past. Instead, we can grab hold of this principle by moving forward in life and being determined to pursue holiness. Remember Paul's words: *"I do not regard myself as having laid hold of it yet."*

Principle Two | One day my son and I were jogging in our neighborhood. I was extremely winded and inclined to stop running. I confessed to him that I wanted to stop and walk the rest of the way. Well, this strong and athletic son of mine decided to put his hand on my shoulder while we're jogging and coach me to keep going. He said my legs would not stop unless I allowed them and that my chest might feel tight, but I would be just fine. He kept repeating this mantra "your legs won't stop unless you let them stop" until we finished the entire route. Although I felt exhilarated for accomplishing the run, I was more tired than an overworked horse. But I did it. I finished the race. My son wouldn't allow me to look back at how much progress we made. He said, "It's not important to know your progress when you still have more distance to run." All he kept telling me was "keep going, keep focused." He was my cheerleader even though I didn't feel like running that distance.

Paul paints a similar picture about how he remains focused on what is ahead of him. He emphatically declares that he doesn't spend time dwelling on his past mistakes or successes because there is more ground ahead to cover. This implies Paul spends his time on matters other than those of the past. "I forget about it," he says, "it's time to move on to something more important." And to Paul, growing in God's grace was the crème de la crème of all his life's accomplishments. How can you make my son's mantra "keep going, keep focused" yours? It is similar to what Paul stated about his life: "*I forget what lies behind and strain forward to what lies ahead.*"

Principle Three | The imagery in Principle Two mirrors that in Principle Three. My guess is Paul isn't being redundant unintentionally. He is trying to make an indelible impact on our minds about forward progress. When I was an active member of Toastmasters, the first rule I learned to giving a good speech was to tell the audience what you wanted them know, tell them again, and then tell then what you just told them. That's a crazy statement but it works. When I followed that rule people would come up to me after my speech and rehash my points. I would light up on the inside, not from their compliments, but when I considered how well that formula works. Using this formula made me appear to be a more experienced speaker. Paul could have been a great Toastmaster because he intrinsically interwove forward progress throughout all three of these principles.

I do not consider that I have made it my own; I forget what lies behind and strain forward to what lies ahead; and I press toward the goal for the prize of the upward call of God in Christ Jesus. These three principles echo one another in calling us to "keep going, keep focused."

Make living with regret a thing of the past!

CHAPTER 11

Fear

A distressing emotion aroused by impending danger,
evil, pain, etc., whether the threat is real or imagined;
the feeling or condition of being afraid

*So do not fear, for I am with you; do not be dismayed,
for I am your God. I will strengthen you and help you;
I will uphold you with my righteous right hand.*
Isaiah 41:10

What an awful and debilitating feeling to be gripped with fear. I can't imagine any other emotion that can be as overpowering and intensely debilitating than fear. Fear is a wakeup call that something or someone has your number. When an activating event that terrifies you strikes your life, you react in fear. Although your knowledge of the matter is limited, your comfort level is low, and even though people try to convince you that you will be fine, you can't help it; fear beats you down. In a unique circumstance when you have to face someone who once controlled, threatened, or hurt you and they are no longer a part of your life, fear swells up in you and grips the living daylights out of your heart. When fear controls your decisions until you can't function, it is at that precise moment that fear has your number. It is stressful, exposing, nonsensical, irrational, real, psychological, experiential, and believable. And in those dark and

Fear

haunting times if you are not careful, fear will come at you.

Fear is an emotion that has eaten my lunch several significant times in my life. It seems like every time I'm confronted with it, I tell myself, "Don't be afraid." But invariably I am overcome with fear. It happened consistently during my cancer treatment journey for over a year. I lived in fear. I might add that during those unusually crazy times, my life was stressful. No sleep, no peace, no solace! It happened unexpectedly as I listened to the oncologist share with me that I had cancer and it was an aggressive type. Honestly, I was so scared and frightened I was shouting at the doctor and accusing her of getting her facts wrong. I told that poor doctor that she must be mistaken and challenged her to go back to the medical records to ensure her information was accurate. I nearly became belligerent with the stunned lady. Was I operating outside my normal way? Yes, yes! When I got a grip on the diagnosis, weeks later an apology was in order from me.

I recall the second time I needed surgery for the cancer, my fear was so overbearing that the oncologist surgeon stared me straight in the eyes and insisted that I find someone else to perform the surgery. He was reacting to my bewildered demeanor and obstinate first impression. And he was absolutely judging me correctly in terms of my behavior. I confessed to Kenneth that here I go again being a pawn of fear. It felt like I couldn't shake it. I had prayed, my pastor and his wife prayed for me, and I implored my family and friends to pray. And most of them will vouch that I asked specifically for prayer over fear. Yet, here are two instances where I am embarrassed by my behavior, retrospectively speaking.

They say, "Perception is reality." Well I perceived that it was my time to depart this life. My thoughts started racing with ideas about drafting a will, funeral plans, and my family's grief. I asked the doctor if I would live or if this particular surgery would end my life. I'm very blessed to have chosen a doctor who was a man of God. He knew he was dealing with an irrational woman who was fear-stricken. Instead of patronizing me, he patiently and kindly explained that doctors can't tell you how a person gets cancer but they have such broad knowledge that treating it is quite successful. He saw fear in my eyes and noticed my inverted shoulders that told him I was running scared.

I must have felt like Elijah after his great victory in the duel between God and the prophets of Baal on Mt. Carmel where in a powerful demonstration God took care of those pseudo-gods when He miraculously consumed Elijah's sacrifice. The contest was centered on establishing before the people who the real god was; Jehovah God or the gods of Baal. By the way, the world's gods are powerless but Jehovah God is all powerful and awesome. All the people witnessing the contest could attest to it. The altars were erected, trenches dug, water poured, sacrificial bulls slain, and prayers offered up. Baal's prophets went first. They prayed but Baal never answered them and no fire rained on their altar. Next, it was Elijah's turn. He erected an altar, dug a trench, sacrificed a bull, and offered up prayers to God. Later, fire consumed his altar and God was recognized as the only true God. It might not have been our definition of a spiritual mega-meeting, but I'm thinking Elijah was sitting real pretty right about this time. He didn't remain feeling victorious particularly when Queen Jezebel inserted herself in the picture and threatened to kill him in the same manner in which he killed the prophets of Baal. That's when our man Elijah was gripped with fear and ran away from Jezebel's threats so fast that it made your head spin.

How can a person be confident in numerous areas but be powerless and fearful at the same time? Elijah was this way. I was (and sometimes still am) this way. He was faithful to God in many areas of his life. Except on the occasion of Jezebel's challenge, experiencing the likelihood of inordinate

Fear

stress, and having a meltdown, Elijah's psyche got the best of him and fear overtook his life. We can only imagine how this downward shift occurred after he learned of Jezebel's threats; the Bible is silent. Yet the outcome was that Elijah sat near a brook crying to God, believing he wanted to die. I have been in that place of fear and sadness as I battled cancer and its stubborn refusal to go away. I believed God would rain down fire on my sacrificial prayers, affirming He is God, He's with me, and that one day cancer will be a rearview memory. Yet, both times when I received the diagnosis, I would flip out on God and run scared just like Elijah. When the doctors recommended I needed surgery, I became motionless because of fear. This pattern repeated itself four times. Yet through it all, God proved to be faithful. We are thousands of years since Elijah, and God's faithfulness has not changed.

How has fear gripped your world? Are you still under its control or have you found the cure-all for its stronghold over you? We are intelligent people who understand that nothing which has power over us disappears from our lives automatically on its own. We might be able to suppress it deep in our minds and hearts, daring it to come to the surface and make a mess of us. We can pretend we are beyond the fear (or any negative emotion) for a long time and that we have disassociated ourselves from it. Or, we might invest time, energy, and money seeking professional help to successfully place the strangler in remission. But unless there is genuine progression toward God to cure the weakness, all the methods we undertake are merely bandaging the wound without addressing the root problem. Isaiah 41:10 begs to differ with us on becoming delivered from our weaknesses through human measures and knowledge. When a person needs deliverance from fear, this verse divulges God's strategy for helping the individual. "Do not fear, for I am with you; do not anxiously look about you, for I am your God. I will strengthen you, surely I will help you; surely I will uphold you with My righteous right hand." God's solution is quite simple and cut-and-dried for such a dominating weakness. He tells us to stop being fearful because He is with us and for us. God's presence allows us to stand on the mountaintop or walk in the valley in every experience we face. This truth is huge for a believer. What other help do you need when one of God's purposes for living in you is to bring you success in Him? Since we can't let go of fear, we must follow the spiritual trail that leads us to our greatest commitment of surrendering it to God.

When fear comes calling on you, you should ensure you have a spiritual Caller ID so that you can place it on hold and conference in the Holy Spirit to speak to your fear. While you and the Holy Spirit are on the phone with "fear," don't poke your two cents into the conversation, just let God handle it. If you could have handled it, you would have done it in the first place. Butt out. Where you can be productive is to ensure you pay your spiritual phone bill in order to keep the lines of communication open between you and God. In other words, the onus is on us to remain connected to God and His responsibility is to lead us successfully through this maze called life.

Why is God so committed to us? He is emphatically committed because He is our Heavenly Father who loves us unconditionally and eternally. He promises to strengthen and help us when we need it. I wanted God to supernaturally heal me of cancer. We enlisted many others to join our petition for God to heal me this way. Yet, when God didn't supernaturally heal my body and I had to undergo the normal adjuvant therapies for cancer, I was fearful while trusting Him simultaneously. Have you ever been there – fearful yet trusting while you relied on the unseen hand of God? Our God can heal supernaturally. He is Almighty God. Therefore, His sovereignty is supreme and without doubt. What I have learned is God can receive more glory when He uses regular, human efforts and ingenuities to work in our lives. He used doctors, chemotherapy, surgeons, and medical drugs to heal me of cancer. I'm living cancer-free. Cancer has made me a stronger influencer in encouraging people to trust God explicitly. He knows what He's up to in your life. He has a plan that is being executed every day and in every experience. Isaiah 41:10 reminds us that God will strengthen us and help us.

Just when God has provided enough assurance in this passage that He is for us and not against us, the verse introduces a final truth that should make the 40-watt light bulb shine like a 120-watt light bulb with confidence in knowing He supports us. The final truth provides further strength and help that specifically come from God's own hands, "I will strengthen you and help you; I will uphold you with my righteous right hand." So far in this passage, God has told us to stop being fearful because He is with us. We need to find peace and safety in that statement: "He is with us!" Next, we should not be troubled over life because He is our God. He has the whole world in His hands. This statement is more than a child's song. It is a powerful declaration of God's ownership over His creation. So don't be overcome by your troubles. He has us in His hands. What does this mean for a child of God? It tells us that He will sustain us not merely in a providential way but a way of special grace. Where God takes care of all of His creation universally, He will sustain His children in ways that are universal but also specifically tailored to our individual needs. We were not created on an assembly line like vehicles being manufactured in a Honda plant. My personality is different from yours and vice-versa. Your life's frames of reference and experience are different than mine. God created us uniquely and individually. So why would He work in your life the same way He does in mine if our needs are different? He won't! And He doesn't! That is why it is an unfair comparison to think that our relationship with God should be like that of another person. We are recipients of a special grace that has a customizable God-shaped design that will only fit one heart, one life, and one mind; yours or mine. That is the strength and help God gives to you and to me; individually but collectively and universally. His ways are mind-boggling, don't you agree?

Special grace is ours, but we also receive special protection and preservation. What is true about the God-shaped pattern that fits our lives uniquely applies the same for His protection and preservation. Over the course of your life, you will be confronted with challenges that apply exclusively to you. God will intervene according to His riches in glory on your behalf. Another person can't assume that the same protection will be provided for him. It most likely can be applicable in another person's life but in reality one truth doesn't hinge on another, meaning God might not determine that a form of protection works for me that works for you. Make this truth applicable for God's preservation of your life. Our lifespan is unique and what we need to accomplish and experience before we die is also unique. The manner in which God finishes the "good work" in us that Paul spoke about in Philippians 1:6 is different from person to person. I think the main and supreme commonality that unites our individual experiences is that we're eternally connected to God through Jesus Christ. He is always with us through the Holy Spirit. Be confident then that God will strengthen you and help you so that you can stand in the grace of God and be obedient to His commands and instructions. Know that you will not fall finally and totally, but that He will preserve you until the end despite your trials and challenges over the course of your life.

Fear

When you are faced with fear, no matter if it is fleeting or horrendous in scope, there is a source of strength who has promised to be with you, help you, strengthen you, and uphold you with His righteous right hand. God has the power to deliver on His promises. Face your fears, don't suppress or deny them. Be stronger than your fear. And never let it dethrone your trust in God. Can God trust you to handle your fears? I believe He can if you give Him full responsibility over whatever is producing the fear.

Fear not! God is by your side!

CHAPTER 12

Love

Because Love is an exhaustive term, the dictionaries didn't do it justice in providing a definition. I confess, this works for me because I can't think of a better definition of love than 1 Corinthians 13

    The magical love story of Danielle and Tony solidifies that not all bad experiences lead to ruin. Their love affair started when Tony was a senior in one of the roughest school districts in his city. In a traditional public school, one where the students can walk freely throughout the campus was not the lay of the land at Tony's school. If students walked to school, as they arrived on the campus, they would be searched by a security guard. Backpacks were opened; items inside the bag were shuffled around and weeded through. The police searched their possessions looking for drugs and weapons. The school was equipped with walk-through and hand-held metal detectors communicating zero tolerance for drugs and weapons. For those students who drove to school, their vehicles were searched and the parking lots were under constant surveillance. There were police security guards who wore taser guns while they visibly patrolled the campus. Among the school's heavy-duty measures was the Random Search Policy that allowed the school to look in students' lockers for drugs, alcohol, or weapons if faculty or security had reasonable suspicion of criminal activity. The entire school district was ground zero for violence, drugs, and crime. The students didn't trust the police who were hired to protect them and ensure there was no violence or crime underway at the school. And the police didn't trust the students because many of them participated in the epidemic of drugs and criminal activities in the community.

One day after Tony had walked to school, he approached the door leading to the gym. There, a man and young girl held him at gunpoint and demanded he give up his money, shoes, jacket, and any other valuables they could find. About the same time as the hold-up, Danielle and her best friend, Winter, were walking toward the same door where Tony was being robbed. When they saw the gun, the girls started screaming and tried to run away. But the robbers yelled for them to stop screaming and not to move another step or they would shoot them. They grabbed the girls' bags and purses and Tony's valuables, and then they ran off. Tony tried to help the girls calm down. By the time the police had arrived, the robbers were gone. The students were about to walk away until the policeman demanded they go to the police station to file a report of the robbery.

Danielle refused to cooperate. She told the policeman that she would just have to deal with it by herself because the last time one of her friends reported a drug dealer at school he was killed. Since Danielle didn't want to file a report Winter decided against it too. The girls tried to convince Tony to move on and forget the incident insisting that he would end up being harassed or even killed just like Danielle's friend. They told him not to trust the police because they were just as crooked as the criminals who robbed them. But it was a matter of principle for Tony and he didn't fear the outcome.

That afternoon after school was over Tony left the campus to walk home when he ran into Danielle again. They talked about what happened that morning and whether Tony was still going to talk to the cops. Before long, they had walked to Danielle's home, talking the entire way without Tony even noticing that her home was in the opposite direction of his. They laughed and talked some more in front of Danielle's home for several hours until Tony decided he had to get home. Danielle asked Tony if she could go with him to the police station and that she would file a report if he did.

The next day Tony walked to Danielle's home so they could walk together to school. Their morning walk turned into a daily routine for the entire school year. By graduation, love was in the air for Tony and Danielle. Neither of the students went to college because they chose to marry in the fall after graduation. They were willing to work anywhere to support themselves and start a family. Danielle adored her man from sun-up to sun-down. They were best friends who had fallen in love despite their tumultuous start where they were robbed at gunpoint.

Young and innocent love is the b-e-s-t! It makes you cry for all the right reasons. It makes you gullible over the simplest things. It causes a man to wear extra cologne and lotion his hands, and a woman to take extra time in the mirror getting dressed. You are sprung! Your life is bombarded by the overcoming power of love. When you think you can slow it down, you just don't think like that anymore. Seriously! You're in love with that person and all you do is think about your special love. Young love often differs from a mature and long-standing love because it is not jaded, sees no faults, doesn't complain, laughs at mistakes, cares less about the person's idiosyncrasies, and holds the person in very high regard at all times. Young love rocks!

What is it about young love that makes a person's heart warm? Whether it is your own personal story or someone else's, your heart simply melts over the euphoric experience. That is why it is a sad commentary when an individual doesn't feel loved or is lonely for love and companionship. Yet when you survey our world look at how many people are living in this category where they have no one special to love, be it a spouse, child, or close friend. People like this end up being love-needy.

    I have been acquainted with a lady whom I considered love needy. She would constantly compliment me about Kenneth. She would tell me that I should be thankful to have a good man because good men are rare nowadays. She has even suggested that I should treat Kenneth extra special because if he were single, he wouldn't stay that way for long. She was someone who had a difficult marriage that terminated in divorce. Believe me, I felt sorry for her situation and I wished her marriage had survived. On those occasions when she had to make it a point to remind me to be extra nice to my husband, it became an annoyance for which I had to find a way to politely ask her to "let it go." I recall there were times where it took God's love to constrain me and to help me keep my mouth closed and not react. Even though I could have validated her assumptions that Kenneth is a good man, God knows there were times when I wanted say, "You don't know a thing about my man; what you have observed is just a fraction of him. So let it go girlfriend." Thank you God for helping me to keep my mouth shut! I have learned that a person who lacks a true loving relationship can be dangerous. That is because living in loneliness and with rejection oftentimes lead to jealousy and cold-heartedness. Since there is a void in their lives, love-needy people can make it very difficult to receive the love for which they are searching and for which they hope happens to them.

    When it comes to love, oftentimes women get a bad rap for being desperate for a man and working aggressively for the "almighty" ring. Some say a single woman earnestly wanting to be married is like an old jalopy. You fix it up, put some new tires on it, give it an oil change, and wash it; then it could last you for years to come. But what I would say is, typically a good woman wants to be married and is looking for a life-long commitment. How dare people make an analogy with women and a jalopy? What's up with that? But you know what? As a woman, it is more troubling to me when women are critical of each other in this area than the bad rap we take with regard to desperately seeking a man. Men desperately seek women too! The playing field is leveled when it comes down to it. Women need to be sensitive to one another by coming alongside that single lady to encourage her, pray with her, and listen to her concerns, especially if she is struggling with loneliness or any negative emotion. I believe caring for single people is a big ministry need in churches nowadays. Singles are certainly one demographic that struggle with loneliness and who need moral support as they face life's challenges. The Body of Christ should view single people, both men and women, as the tremendous asset that they are to church. From their vantage point, this is the group that can shoulder the responsibility for special missions and projects. They are able to care for the church's needs at odds times and rare occasions. Churches are all the more better if single ministries are vibrant and engaging.

Remember the story of Danielle and Tony, the young and in love, who were innocent and not jaded? The making of their love story gives us a weak but positive glimpse of God's love for us. In the great Love Chapter of the Bible – 1 Corinthians 13 – God gives us a precious but powerful love declaration for the ages. Generations will live and generations will die as long as God sustains this world, but His love declaration in 1 Corinthians 13 is everlasting. Consider this point and beyond the final leg of EMOTIONS. I plan on engrossing your mind with my layman's exposition of The Love Chapter.

Here we go...

Are you multilingual and take great pride in your linguistic abilities? Are you eloquent, fluent, and can speak

Love

in ways that are angelic but you fail in loving God, others, and yourself? Don't be too enamored with your achievements because God characterizes you as someone full of hot wind and useless talk that neither impresses nor pleases Him.

Have you been blessed with the gift of prophecy? Do you have insight on spiritual significance? Are you keenly knowledgeable about God's word and His ways? Are you counted among the most faithful of God's children who could be placed in Hebrews 11 with other Faith Giants of the Bible? You could perform many wonderful works in Jesus' name? You are a conduit for helping others overcome great challenges through your faith, but you lack love for God, others, and yourself? Watch out! God has something to say to you. He wants you to know that you are nothing without His love.

Are you an altruistic person who relishes helping the downcast and poor? Will you agree to such a noble act as giving your body to science when you die or donating your organs to someone in need? Do you tithe faithfully as well as give consistently to your favorite charities or ministries and insist on your tax write-off and thank-you letters? Do you take the time to ensure the powers-that-be realize your contributions or support but you are stingy with your love for God, others, and yourself? The news flash from above is without God's love you might gain recognition before men but with the Father you have gained nothing.

Here is what God values about true love. His standard for love must be expressed with patience, leaving the impetuous and flighty propensities out of the equation. The love that meets his approval is kind not hostile, not aggressive, nor overbearing, or controlling. The famous words of Elvis Presley, "Love me tender, love me sweet, never let me go," hints the right tune to God's love. True, Godly love isn't associated with greed, jealousy, or envy. You can't love another person if you can't be satisfied or have contentedness in your relationships. God alone possesses a holy jealousy which He carries toward His children who are His prized possession. He is jealous for us in an inexpressible and Godly way. When love is authentic, a person will never boast about the quality of his love. And they surely won't leverage their love to announce or publicize how well they love, the numerous instances in which they have shown love, or who benefits from their love. Their heart will be able to love without advertising it in a boastful way. And finally, love is proud in how it cares for a heart, how it protects a life, and how it is fully and unconditionally committed. But it is not proud with arrogance, conceit, self-righteousness, or self-serving because all of these characteristics are oxymoronic when it comes to God's love.

*If you ain't got love,
you ain't got nothin'*

(Smile with me, I couldn't resist using slang.)

What's love got to do with it? Love is the foundation that undergirds why we are reconciled with God. It doesn't dishonor Him, His creation, or His people. The Christian journey can be considered arduous given the example Jesus set. He was meek and lowly in heart, yet Jesus was simultaneously the living embodiment of power and manliness. He didn't cower in the face of challenges, but He didn't defend his character when it was being assassinated. He rarely got angry except for the times when He had to address blatant wickedness and disrespect to His Father. Yet He's God and even in those cases His love still abounded. We, as a people, are a work in progress in one, if not all, of these areas.

We honor God, Jesus, and the Holy Spirit because we have been convinced that our God deserves the honor

Love

due His name. When we honor God we express His love. When we seek another person's interest or God's causes before our own, we are expressing God's love. When we are level-headed, slow to anger, and quick to keep quiet, we are expressing God's love. And when we don't play "tit for tat" with people who offend us, mistreat us, or even spitefully use us, we've got it. We have God's love living on the inside. Now does it make sense to you why the dictionary couldn't provide us with an exhaustive definition for love? Do you realize this is the longest chapter in this book namely because we are talking about L-O-V-E? What other emotion can turn your life upside down and inside out like LOVE?

What makes love work? Love loves righteousness and the corollary is it hates evil. Godly love will turn off evil influences. That is a daunting prospect because our world is saturated with evil influences. I could spend the rest of this chapter enumerating one evil influence after another. However, the litmus test for knowing if something is evil or sinful is spiritual conviction. When the Holy Spirit convicts us that something is evil or a sin, we must respond accordingly to His instructions, whether or not others agree with us. What is more, we might have to let our feelings catch up with our conviction. Sometimes, the two are not in sync when God brings spiritual conviction or revelation to our lives. When conviction comes, true love won't despise instruction but will rejoice over the truth. Consequently, Godly love <u>always</u> (I rarely use absolute statements such as "always" or "every time", but I can break that rule when it comes to the consistency of God's love) protects, trusts, hopes, and preserves truth and life.

God's love amazes me. Does it amaze you? Who other than our Great Father could have codified a picture of love such as the one He painted in the Love Chapter through the inspired Apostle Paul? He acknowledges that love is failproof. In other words, if Godly love is your foundation you should never second-guess its longevity or preeminence. However, we should be cognizant that great religious practices such as prophecies will cease, speaking in tongues will be silenced, and knowledge will end when this life is over. They weren't established to last forever – just love.

What did Isaiah, Jeremiah, Ezekiel, and Daniel have in common? Besides being men of righteousness, they were anointed prophets whom God chose to be his mouthpiece to speak forth His messages to His people, the Jews, concerning the nation of Judah, the city of Jerusalem, the Gentiles, and the whole house of Israel. Their prophesies were fulfilled according to God's divine plan, except for the last-day predictions about events that will take place on the earth preceding Jesus' second coming. In the greatest acts of this gift, God planned for prophecy to be limited even though many lives have been greatly blessed and preserved through this special gift. However, it will not last forever.

Many believers espouse speaking in tongues as God's love language to lead, edify, encourage, and correct the church. There are some believers whose lives have been blessed by utilizing the gift of tongues to enhance their walk with God, strengthen their faith, and improve their prayer life. Whether you believe this gift is manifested through an unknown language, one that is of a heavenly form or through interpreting a foreign translatable language, speaking in tongues is a viable gift and the Bible substantiates its legitimacy. Yet, the purpose for speaking in tongues and its usefulness will be silenced one day.

There are all types of knowledge in our world, but the knowledge I want to focus on comes from God's Word. Bible scholars, preachers, teachers, or people who have studied the Bible with a high-level commitment, understand that their knowledge is imparted to them by God's Spirit. They know that God's inspired Word stands as the solid source of all right knowledge. Beyond the basics of life, spiritual knowledge is what we need for survival. Each of us needs spiritual understanding and insight into that special knowledge revealed only by God Himself.

Knowledge is something we can obtain instantaneously in the world today. We don't have to wait anymore for what we need to know about any subject. All we have to do is download the file, search for it on the Internet, or listen to it through an audio device. In the midst of society's knowledge explosion, there is a tremendous need for Biblical literacy. It would seem that since we are technologically advanced with access to any conceivable source that people would have a greater degree of competency in God's word. But oftentimes we have placed the Bible on the backburner of our life where we use it if we need God for a specific reason. All and all, knowledge is temporary and short-lived and will end one day. But God's knowledge is everlasting and sustaining far beyond this life and into our glorious new life. When God's love is revealed in our hearts we soon realize that we are unable to fully comprehend the enormity of our Father's love for us and His world. He has imparted only a portion of the story on which we can salivate until He reveals it all. We must continue to trust our faithful God's plan to reveal His love through and through, to show us its completeness on the other side of eternity when this side of life is over.

Do you remember when you first accepted Jesus Christ? Maybe your experience is similar to mine. I have always had knowledge of Jesus because I was brought up in church, attended church schools through college, and most of my friends were Christians. I was probably at a disadvantage in terms of fully realizing that bright day when I asked Him to come into my life. Many church people who have a rich Christian heritage find it difficult to pinpoint the day they became born-again. In fact, when God rocked my world at thirteen, in retrospect I didn't fully understand it. Although my life was in a forward-progress motion I had a difficult time differentiating good from bad or understanding why bad things happened to good people, especially me, and why I should love people who didn't deserve my love. I was just a baby in Christ who God was growing up in a very measured and methodical way. Trust me, becoming a mature Christian, whom I consider myself, is a journey filled with many failures and some coveted successes. We've all been there. Yes, every mature Christian has had to pay the price to grow up in the Lord.

As such, God reminds us of our immaturity in the Love Chapter. For one thing, when we were young in Christ our language was indicative of our childish ways, and our thoughts needed to be replaced with what Paul calls "virtuous thinking" in Philippians 4:8. Subsequently, as mature children of God, we have learned through the leadership of the Holy Spirit that we can no longer act like a child. In fact, childish things are unattractive to us. It makes sense to me why God would juxtapose how love is partially revealed on this side of eternity versus the next life. Is it possible that He would have blown our minds had He given us the whole shebang now? Let's consider the brightest of us, and I would put Paul at the top of the list. He confessed that he couldn't fathom the breadth, depth, and height of our God's love toward us. Why couldn't Paul comprehend it? The Word says, in verse 9 of the Love Chapter that God only gave us part of the Love story, and He restates this reality in verse 12. We don't need to know the rest of the story; all we have to do is trust the powerful and mighty hands of Almighty God. In that glorious day when He reveals the entire story, the Love Chapter surmises that "then we will know everything God has intended for us to have and experience about His love." We will be fully capable of handling it!

But until then, until that day, that glorious day when Jesus comes back to earth for us, Christian virtues and practices are important in our relationship with Him. The first righteous practice, faith, requires us to walk and sometimes crawl through the mountains and valleys without interrogating God on the "whys" and "hows." To please God in this life, you must walk by faith and not by sight. The second righteous practice that must continue until Jesus comes again is having Hope. That is, hope expects us to keep on believing we are irreplaceable to God, that He will complete the perfect work in us that He began at the foundation of the world. And last but not least, love is the foundation by which we remain at peace with God and one another.

The Christian virtue that trumps all other practices, gifts, callings, works, and the like is none other than love.

If you are living in loneliness or boredom or you need more patience; if you are happy with your life or living in the throes of rejection; if you have sweet peace with God and in your life, or you can't tell your night from day because depression has taken over your world; if you are guilt-stricken for a wrong or a sin; if you vow to be courageous in the midst of your challenges; if you live with regrets of your past; if fear has a hold on you and you won't let it go, may God's love constrain you and keep you ever near His heart until His Son returns for you. There, my friend, you will have no worries because Love will reign supreme!

Now, may I direct your minds to the inspiring verses from the great Love Chapter of 1 Corinthians 13? No explanations needed...

–1 Corinthians 13

> *If I speak in the tongues of men or of angels,* but do not have love, *I am only a resounding gong or a clanging cymbal. If I have the gift of prophecy and*

can fathom all mysteries and all knowledge, and if I have a faith that can move mountains, but do not have love, *I am nothing. If I give all I possess to the poor and give over my body to hardship that I may boast,* but do not have love, *I gain nothing.*

Love is patient, love is kind. It does not envy, it does not boast, it is not proud. It does not dishonor others, it is not self-seeking, it is not easily angered, it keeps no record of wrongs. Love does not delight in evil but rejoices with the truth. It always protects, always trusts, always hopes, always perseveres. Love never fails. *But where there are prophecies, they will cease; where there are tongues they will be stilled; where there is knowledge, it will pass away.*

For we know in part and we prophesy in part, but when completeness comes, what is in part disappears. When I was a child, I talked like a child, I thought like a child, I reasoned like a child. When I became a man, I put the ways of childhood behind me. For now we see only a reflection as in a mirror; then we shall see face to face. Now I know in part; then I shall know fully, even as I am fully known. And now these three remain: faith, hope and love. But the greatest of these is love.

God is love and love comes from Him. Amen!

Notes

1. Charminghealth.com. 2000-2009: Loneliness or Feeling *Lonely Owing to Emotional Imbalance*. http://www.charminghealth.com/applicability/loneliness.htm, 4.
2. Modern Peacemakers - Mother Teresa, *Caring for the World's Poor* (page 63). http://www.elcaminosantiago.com/PDF/Book/Mother_Teresa_-_Caring_For_The_Worlds_Poor.pdf, 5.
3. Definition of Boredom, Chapter 2, is defined by Encyclopedia.com. http://www.encyclopedia.com/topic/Boredom.aspx, 13.
4. Refer to Psychology Today, *The New Resilience*, May 3, 2010, by Douglas LaBier, Ph.D. http://www.psychology-today.com/blog/the-new-resilience/201005/feeling-bored-work-three-reasons-why-and-what-can-free-you, 14.
5. Refer to USA Today. http://www.usatoday.com/educate/ondcp/lessons/Activity2.pdf, 15.
6. Online Parallel Bible: *Matthew Henry's Concise Commentary on the Bible*. http://mhc.biblecommenter.com/matthew/5.htm, 34.
7. Biblos.com: *Gills Exposition of the Entire Bible Commentary*. http://bible.cc/matthew/5-5.htm, 35.

8. The National Geographic Daily News, March 28, 2011. http://news.nationalgeographic.com/news/2011/03/110328-romantic-rejection-pain-brain-scans-mri-health-science/, 41.
9. Pathoes.com: *Seeking the Peace of Christ: Christianity and Peacemaking*, by Rev. Dr. Mark D. Roberts. http://www.patheos.com/blogs/markdroberts/series/seeking-the-peace-of-christ-christianity-and-peacemaking, 54.
10. Ranking America's Mental Health: *An Analysis of Depression Across the States.* http://www.mental-healthamerica.net/go/state-ranking, 56.
11. PsychologyToday.com: *What is Courage? Existential Lessons From the Cowardly Lion, Psychology Today*, Dr. Stephen A. Diamond, April 28, 2011. http://www.psychologytoday.com/blog/evil-deeds/201104/what-is-courage-existential-lessons-the-cowardly-lion, 69.
12. Chapters 1 and 3 to 11 include a definition at the beginning of the chapter. The source for all definitions comes from http://dictionary.reference.com.

About The Author

Vanessa Hall is the founder of **Grace Matters Ministries**. The ministry exists to proclaim that salvation is a free gift through Jesus Christ, and to strengthen believers' faith in remaining committed to Jesus in this generation.

Through Grace Matters Ministries, Vanessa hosts *Grace Matters* radio broadcast. It is a weekly program that airs on 100.7 FM on Sundays at 4:00 p.m., serving the Houston metropolitan area. Broadcasts can also be accessed at www.kkht.com or through Vanessa's website at http://www.grace-matters.com. You can also listen to podcasts through Grace Matters website on the **RADIO and SPEAKING** page.

Another facet of the ministry is the lively presentation **Disgrace To His Grace**. D2G, as Vanessa calls it, is an eye-opening journey of five steps where she takes you from our common place of Disgrace to that undeserving place of God's amazing Grace.

When Vanessa isn't speaking or engaged in radio, she spends time blogging daily devotionals, which she calls **Vanessa's Easy Reading Blogs**. These short and to-the-point devotions can be digested in less than two minutes. They are published Monday through Friday. You can read these nuggets of encouragement and wisdom through her website on the **BLOG** page.

One of this author's greatest passions can be observed through her two Bible study programs. She leads a monthly Women Ministries Bible study at her home church – North

Central – in Spring, Texas. And she leads a private ladies Bible study in her home every other Friday.

Vanessa is currently working through academic studies to becoming an ordained minister.

She is married to Kenneth Hall and the couple lives in Spring, Texas. They have three adult sons, Andrew, age 26, and Jordan and Joshua (twins), age 20.

Do you need a speaker?

If you would like Vanessa Hall to speak to your group, church, or event, contact Grace Matters Ministries at 281-288-8751, email at info@grace-matters.com, or visit the Contact Page on the website at www.grace-matters.com.

Do you want additional books?

Additional copies of this book are available at:

Grace Matters Ministries: www.grace-matters.com
FB: http://www.facebook.com/VanessaHallMinistries
Xulon Website Page: http://www.xulonpress.com/bookstore/bookdetail.php?PB_ISBN=9781622309245.

Available through: Amazon.com, Barnesandnoble.com, and Google Books.

CPSIA information can be obtained at www.ICGtesting.com
Printed in the USA
LVOW130329110912

298097LV00001B/5/P